The Media Globe

The Media Globe

Trends in International Mass Media

Edited by Lee Artz and Yahya R. Kamalipour

ROWMAN & LITTLEFIELD PUBLISHERS, INC.
Lanham • Boulder • New York • Toronto • Plymouth, UK

ROWMAN & LITTLEFIELD PUBLISHERS, INC.

Published in the United States of America
by Rowman & Littlefield Publishers, Inc.
A wholly owned subsidiary of The Rowman & Littlefield Publishing Group, Inc.
4501 Forbes Boulevard, Suite 200, Lanham, Maryland 20706
www.rowmanlittlefield.com

Estover Road, Plymouth PL6 7PY, United Kingdom

British Library Cataloguing in Publication Information Available

Library of Congress Cataloging-in-Publication Data

The media globe : trends in international mass media / edited by Lee Artz and
Yahya R. Kamalipour.
    p. cm.
  Includes bibliographical references and index.
  ISBN-13: 978-0-7425-4093-4 (cloth : alk. paper)
  ISBN-10: 0-7425-4093-6 (cloth : alk. paper)
  ISBN-13: 978-0-7425-4094-1 (pbk. : alk. paper)
  ISBN-10: 0-7425-4094-4 (pbk. : alk. paper)
  1. Communication, International. 2. Globalization. I. Artz, Lee. II. Kamalipour,
Yahya R.
  P96.I5M424 2007
  302.2—dc22

                                                              2006023836

Printed in the United States of America

⊗™ The paper used in this publication meets the minimum requirements of
American National Standard for Information Sciences—Permanence of Paper
for Printed Library Materials, ANSI/NISO Z39.48-1992.

Contents

Foreword

One of the most popular buzzwords of our age is *globalization*. It also is a strongly contested concept with different meanings for different authors. Although it is commonly used in the singular, it would be more precise to refer to *globalizations*. In today's world one can observe the globalization of health risks through HIV infection or avian flu, the globalization of ecological threats, the globalization of economic interdependence, the globalization of finance, or the globalization of cultural commodities and lifestyles. Common to all these globalizations is a rapid transnational expansion of events and agents that were formerly contained within national borders. This is manifest in the world of the media where we can observe a fast and effective transnationalization and de-nationalization of operations by the leading actors.

Basic to globalizations is the ideology of globalism. This represents a set of moral standards that legitimize the direction of globalizations. There are different schools of globalism. Dominant is the neoliberal variant, which sanctions the unimpeded movement of investment and trade across the globe. In fact this globalism is a crude form of economic determinism that conveniently but incorrectly refers to Adam Smith as its inspirational source. Smith's moralistic thoughts about a free market, based upon the notion of general welfare, seem to fit better with an alternative globlalism that opposes neoliberalism. The protagonists of this globalism, who are often and deceptively called antiglobalists, put people and human rights at the core of their preferred global arrangement.

The adjustments that take place around the media globe are most often driven by neoliberal globalism. The chapters in this book document this state of affairs with a good deal of evidence. One regrettable aspect of this trend is that key actors show little if any concern for the consequences of their operations to such general welfare notions as freedom of information, accessibility of knowledge, or diversity of cultural contents. In most cases, the transnational operators will claim this is precisely what they promote and foster: the free and diversified flow of informational and cultural products and services.

The neoliberal ideologues pretend to march behind the banner of freedom. This requires their rather limited interpretation of "freedom" as the lifting of regulations for cross-border trading. However, freedom is more than a notion found in trade-law books. In the language of human rights, freedom refers to the right to freedom of expression and the right to freedom of information—to the fullest possible and affordable access to information, to the free choice of sources, and to the maximum diversity of information and cultural expressions. This is the kind of freedom that major globalizing companies such as Microsoft, Yahoo, and Google are willing to negotiate away in their recent deals with the Chinese government.

The authors of the chapters that follow show that today's global media trends pose a serious threat to the basic principles for media practices adopted by the world community in 1948 through the *Universal Declaration of Human Rights*.

The book that is before you is an excellent source of empirical documentation and theoretical analysis on the most pertinent media practices that are at work around the globe. The collected texts address global, regional, and national situations. Through these detailed descriptions of key trends, this book provides the reader with a near-comprehensive overview of media practices in the world.

As a long-time teacher in the field of international communication, I am forever searching for accessible, useful, and up-to-date textbooks on the matter. The "mother of all textbooks" does not exist and probably never will due to the enormous complexity, broadness, and rapid developments in the field. It is therefore prudent of the editors to refer to trends in international mass media practices. In various chapters the reader will find the authors write about the media in Africa, which are in a state of flux, the Arab television industry, which will remain in flux in the near future, and the European television market, which continues to undergo rapid change. Trends will change and this cannot be the last textbook for students' reading, but the book is likely to last for a considerable time to come.

The Media Globe provides an excellent starting point for thinking about media practices in the future tense. This is an exercise that is sorely needed in communication studies. At such conferences as the World Future Society, which convenes professionals from many disciplines to develop foresight, innovation, and strategy, communication scholars are usually in short supply, if they participate at all. Few of the curricula in communication studies around the world deal seriously with future studies. Yet, most of what will happen to communication processes, communication institutions, and media practices will obviously occur in the future. The field of future studies has now moved beyond the stage of totally nonplausible projections and forecasts into a rich domain of solid methodological and theoretical thinking on the future. If we took this intellectual challenge seriously we would not forever be taken by surprise when confronted with the future effects of current trends.

To understand the topography of today's media globe, the contributors to this book provide competent guidance and stimulate the reader to explore new territories. Like those who manufactured the first globe some four centuries ago in the German town of Nuremberg as a model of the world, the authors of *The Media Globe* have constructed a model that invites us to criticism, reflection, and action.

As writer of a foreword, I need to be careful to avoid the trap bedeviling many chairs in academic conferences who speak at length to introduce their speakers and wear out the audiences before the keynote commences. The following pages speak for themselves and I invite you to peruse them and judge for yourselves.

Cees J. Hamelink
Professor Emeritus
University of Amsterdam

Introduction

Lee Artz and Yahya R. Kamalipour

The Media Globe: Trends in International Mass Media is conceived and organized to provide an up-to-date, multifaceted perspective about the trends and media practices in various parts of the world. Given the rapid consolidation of international media, the subsequent reform of international media regulatory agencies, and the continuing deregulation, privatization, and commercialization of national and local media, the editors—as well as the publisher—saw an urgent need for a reassessment of the state of international communication.

In 2006, a handful of giant media corporations—TimeWarner, Disney, News Corporation, Bertelsmann, and Viacom—monopolized the entertainment and information industry in the United States and many regions of the world. In the Western hemisphere, the economic success of media corporations is frequently attributed to the enthusiastic reception of international audiences to Disney's animated features, MTV videos, sports programming, game shows, and other media commodities. However, few have seriously considered how rapid changes in global news and entertainment production and distribution are affecting the values, knowledge, and norms of other cultures. Industry studies on advertising, public relations, television programming, and media expansion reflexively assume the Western corporate and consumer model best serves public information needs in the United States and elsewhere. Recent critical theoretical work is based largely on case studies and fieldwork of media and communication practices from the 1980s and 1990s that are no longer operative. As a consequence, the balance sheet on international communication is inaccurate and dated, even as change in media practice accelerates and

1

becomes more complex. Several books are likely necessary to stay abreast of changes and consequences, but first and foremost, an informative overview—offered in this book—is necessary and can help frame the issues and trends that may need more specific study.

This book project grew out of a rather casual conversation that the editors had following the 2004 Global Fusion Conference in St. Louis, Missouri. The conversation was about globalization forces and international media expansion, which together continue to alter social norms and cultural conventions throughout the world. As is often the case, casual conversations tend to lead to serious and meaningful endeavors, and the publication of this volume is, indeed, a case in point.

Broadly conceived and regionally organized, this volume is intended to

1. provide observations and insights on the emerging practices and patterns of African, Asian, Middle Eastern, European, and Latin American media;
2. identify existing and developing issues and problems in international media communication and their potential impact on democratic communication;
3. assess the current tensions between ongoing global media practices and local and regional cultural norms;
4. identify and assess how various theoretical approaches (e.g., globalization, hybridity, hegemony, cultural imperialism, and world systems theory) provide useful frames for understanding current global media practices in different geographic regions; and
5. consider possible alternative scenarios for global communication based on various local, regional, and national cultural norms and practices.

To provide an overview of contemporary international media practices and their impact on different geographic regions, this book consists of seven chapters written by leading media scholars who are knowledgeable and informed about contemporary political conditions and media practices in each region of the world, including Africa, Asia, Australia, Europe, the Middle East, Latin America, and North America. Each chapter includes an appendix identifying some of the major media in the region. Below is a brief description of each chapter:

CHAPTER 1: AFRICA:
LIFE IN THE MARGINS OF GLOBALIZATION

In this chapter, Lyombe Eko argues that since the end of the Cold War, the African media landscape has been markedly affected by the interplay and coalescence of multiple forces: globalization and Internet connectivity and the concomitant increased interconnection with the rest of the world, as well as democratization, liberalization, deregulation, and commercialization. Eko also analyzes media trends in Africa within the framework of globalization, media hegemony, and power. His main contention is that the African media are in a state of flux, hence they show the following trends: (1) World Bank and IMF-driven liberalization, deregulation, and privatization of telecommunications and broadcasting have led to commercialization; (2) the increasingly active role the United States and European powers play on the African broadcast scene has led to a marked increase in international broadcast surrogacy on the continent; (3) liberalization and democratization have given rise to a vibrant, irreverent, satirical press that is a thorn in the flesh of many an authoritarian government; and (4) Africans are beginning to reinvent the Internet and other information and communication technologies to suit African cultural and political realities.

CHAPTER 2: ASIA: THE HOLLYWOOD FACTOR

In this chapter, Kuldip Rampal contends that film industries in several Asian countries are in the process of reinventing themselves as traditional approaches to filmmaking become increasingly unviable economically. Rampal attributes the declining box office associated with traditional filmmaking to economic and cultural globalization, occurring with the expansion of democracy around the world, forces which bring Western cultural influences and entertainment styles to increasingly economically well-off and educated people in Asian countries. Rampal explains the appeal and adoption of these styles in the Asian film industries within the framework of the theories of cultural dependency and media evolution. He argues that there is a growing "Hollywoodization" of Asian films— marked by themes built around sex, violence, action, drugs, and alcohol use. However, evidence indicates that Hollywood is getting Asianized to some degree, showing influences from the Japanese, Korean, Hong Kong, and Indian movie industries. Profit-driven cost concerns are pushing Hollywood to outsource production and postproduction work. This cultural and economic symbiosis between Asia and America is likely to grow and to serve the entertainment and cultural needs of elite cosmopolitan audiences that are open to consuming and appreciating foreign cultural influences without entirely rejecting their own.

CHAPTER 3: EUROPE: TELEVISION IN TRANSITION

In this chapter, Jeanette Steemers contends that the media market in Europe is distinct and complex because of its enormous cultural and linguistic diversity, but that it is also a market undergoing rapid change. In spite of audiences' undoubted preferences for domestic programming, national boundaries are increasingly giving way in terms of ownership, operational practices, technology, and audience experiences. This, Steemers suggests, has been demonstrated by the proliferation of globally distributed television formats and channels since the late 1990s, which demonstrate the global interconnectedness and experience of television.

She charts the institutional development of television in Europe and explains how commercial television and consumer-demand priorities have superseded public service and supply concerns connected with television's role as a forum serving the interests of citizenship and democracy.

CHAPTER 4: THE MIDDLE EAST: TRANSNATIONAL ARAB TELEVISION

Marwan Kraidy and Joe F. Khalil focus on the Arab television industry and describe the contours of some ongoing transformations, even as programming and production trends remain fluid. Following a brief discussion of the historical and general background of the Arab television industry, the authors identify and analyze established patterns and emerging trends in the industry, including (1) the emergence of regionalization, (2) the advent of niche media markets, (3) the rise of "networks," and (4) the predominance of genres such as talk shows, reality television, and video clips. Kraidy and Khalil synthesize their findings and set some parameters for research on Arab television in the coming decade, with the caveat that in the rapidly changing Arab television industry, current patterns may change in the near future. The appendixes present vital information about the industry.

CHAPTER 5: LATIN AMERICA: MEDIA CONGLOMERATES

In this chapter, José-Carlos Lozano observes the contemporary media scene in Latin America. Since the 1980s, he notes, several scholars in the field of international communication have questioned the assertions of cultural imperialists about a strong dependency of Latin American audiovisual media on U.S. media content. Using concepts like "cultural proximity," "cultural discount," and "cultural-linguistic markets," these researchers have pointed to the increase in the national production of television programs in many Latin American countries in recent decades, and to the success of regional imports between these countries. Lozano discusses the relevance of these concepts to the contemporary reality of the Latin American audiovisual space. He then (1) reviews recent developments in the consolidation and expansion of Latin American media conglomerates and their links and alliances with other regional and transnational groups, (2) studies current flows of television content within Latin American countries, tracking the volume of regional exports and imports, and (3) examines the ratings of these imports in different countries of the region, comparing them with local productions. Lozano concludes that there is a need to question celebratory and uncritical approaches, and to establish a dialogue between advocates of the "cultural proximity" argument and advocates of the political economy approach to reach more balanced, holistic descriptions and explanations about the current situation in the Latin American audiovisual space.

CHAPTER 6: AUSTRALIA: MEDIA AND GLOBALIZATION

In this chapter, Alan Knight acquaints readers with the Australian media scene, which is heavily influenced by Rupert Murdoch's News Corporation. The News Corporation became the first fully transnationalized media consortium by shaking off the vestiges of its Australian corporate origins and locating itself squarely in U.S. markets. Knight argues that in less than half a century, Murdoch and his family have transformed News Corporation from a regional Australian newspaper to a horizontally and vertically integrated multimedia giant that markets its cultural packages across the United States, Europe, Asia, and the Pacific. In this process, Australia, whose media are increasingly dominated by News Corporation products that include newspapers, cinema, music, cable television, and sport, has become a regional conduit taking these products to even more remote corners of the corporate empire. The author examines how the new world order impacts Australia's media practices and politics and imposes new stereotypes and cultural norms.

CHAPTER 7: THE CORPORATE MODEL
FROM NATIONAL TO TRANSNATIONAL

In this final chapter, coeditor Lee Artz provides not only a succinct wrap-up but also examines the model of media deregulation, privatization, and commercialization that was politically codified with two historic policy decisions: the *1996 Telecommunications Act* of the U.S. Congress, which removed the last obstacles to corporate consolidation of the media in the United States, and the 1995 founding of the World Trade Organization, which further institutionalized the corporate media "free-flow" model as essential to the new world order of transnational capital. He notes that the seventy-year wave of corporate media activity in the United States previews the trajectory of international media structures, activities, and programming. Artz contends that across and around this media globe, the new model will be transnational—a formation of transnational corporations with joint-venture class interests that supersede their national and cultural homes, with communication content that may be localized as an expression of their commercialization and market-driven goals. Artz thereby corrects the insufficient recognition of class power in various explanations of hybridity, cultural proximity, and glocalization. Emerging transnational media will further the process of institutionalization by socially and culturally advancing news, information, advertising, and entertainment that reinforce and promote the neoliberal market policies, norms, and values.

As globalization proceeds, the central role of media and media technology therein becomes ever more apparent and the need for a book addressing the ramifications of media globalization at home and abroad becomes clearly evident. Hence, this book is intended for scholars, researchers, and students of media and international studies, as well as media professionals, instructors, researchers, and importantly, the general international public.

We all experience daily the impact of globalization, from Chicago and New York, to Bombay, Rio, and local villages in China and the Ukraine. Our task as observers, researchers, and citizens is to note the trends and impulses in media globalization and to describe, predict, and alert our fellow world citizens of the choices we have and choices we need to create. This book is one contribution to that inquiry and conversation—it is a request to join us in dialogue about what kind of world we desire and deserve and how we might create a more democratic, human-centered media globe.

1

Africa: Life in the
Margins of Globalization

Lyombe Eko

Uganda received a crash course in freedom of speech and of the press in, of all places, the bars of Kampala, the capital. As a result of media liberalization carried out under World Bank and International Monetary Fund (IMF) economic restructuring programs, tens of broadcasting licenses were issued to religious, communal, and ethnic groups, as well as media entrepreneurs (Ogundimu 1996). Two results of this liberalization were broadcast commercialization and cutthroat competition. When revelations of real or imagined government corruption, ineptitude, and scandal, as well as American-style global–Top 40 music, were not enough to attract and hold audiences, some newly licensed FM stations reinvented radio through a novel free speech phenomenon—barroom broadcasting, or *Ekimeeza* (literally, *beer-hall talk*) (Ibelema et al. 2004).

As politicians, including President Yoweri Museveni, took to the airwaves to campaign for political office, radio stations saw an opportunity to increase their ratings. Many headed for the bars. They often chose a moderator—usually a lawyer, politician, or other well-known figure—and made their microphones available to all and sundry. The resulting alcohol-fueled debates, which took place in a mixture of dialects and languages, were broadcast live. All topics were fair game. The government was often on the receiving end of political attacks. Before too long the phenomenon had spread like wildfire across the broadcast spectrum. Some stations started *Ekimeeza* in Luganda, the language spoken by a large section of the Ugandan population.

When debaters started being disrespectful or insulting toward the president and other government officials, a jittery Ugandan government threatened to ban live broadcasts of barroom debates on the grounds that broadcast licenses do not allow such live outside broadcasts. Many politicians and the press of course saw this as an attempt to censor the free-form political debates. Nevertheless, threats of libel suits and governmental pressure forced these stations to tone the debates down (Ibelema et al. 2004).

The Ugandan free speech experiment is an exemplar of the fundamental changes that have swept the mass media in Africa since the early 1990s. Indeed, the fall of the Berlin Wall in 1989 and the collapse of the Soviet Union in 1991 changed Africa's geostrategic importance. As the sole superpower, the United States no longer needed to prop up authoritarian regimes on the continent as a counter to Soviet expansionism. Many authoritarian regimes were left to fend for themselves. The result was a period of democratization and liberalization (Ihonvbere 1997; Ihonvbere and Mbaku 2003). Hundreds of newspapers, tabloids, magazines, newssheets, and satirical publications of all political hues, journalistic competence, and ethnic affiliations sprouted like mushrooms across sub-Saharan Africa (Eko 2003a; Geslin 2002).

The aim of this chapter is to survey the major trends across the African media landscape in the post–Cold War period, from the perspective of globalization, hegemony, and power. I will explore the impact on the continent of globalization and its associated power dynamics within the broadcast media, newspapers, and the Internet. I contend the African media reflect power differentials both within individual countries and between the continent and the rich, industrialized countries of the West. Furthermore, I contend that globalization, deregulation, and commercialization of the media in Africa are the result of the asymmetrical power relations between African countries and former colonial powers, the United States, and the United Nations. This chapter seeks to answer the question: How do globalization, hegemony, and asymmetrical power relations impact the media in Africa?

I contend the media in Africa show the following trends: (1) World Bank and IMF-driven liberalization, deregulation, and privatization of telecommunications and broadcasting have led to commercialization; (2) the increasingly active role the United States and European powers play on the African broadcast scene has led to a marked increase in international broadcast surrogacy on the continent; (3) liberalization and democratization have given rise to a vibrant, irreverent, satirical press that is a thorn in the flesh of many an authoritarian government; and (4) Africans are beginning to reinvent the Internet and other information and communication technologies to suit their cultural and political realities.

THEORETICAL PERSPECTIVE:
GLOBALIZATION, HEGEMONY, AND POWER

The phenomenon of globalization has been variously described as increased global interconnectedness, interdependence, and interaction among peoples, cultures, and civilizations (Held and McGrew 2002) and as global "informational capitalism marked by knowledge creation, economic productivity, and the fluid flow of information and financial capital" (Castells 2000, p. 20). Globalization or neoliberal globalization is said to have normalized Anglo-American individualism, competition, deregulation, liberalization, privatization, neomercantilism, and minimal state intervention in the economy (Mittelman 2004). Globalization has also been defined as the cultural expression of politics and economics through common solidarities, habits, standards of behavior, and norms. In short, globalization creates a common culture, one that presupposes a common knowledge system transmitted across vast distances by the transnational media and mass travel (Bamyeh 2000, p. 89). The most visible manifestations of cultural globalization are American. These include films, television programs, computer software, video games, iPods, Coca Cola, McDonald's, CNN, the Marlboro man, basketball, baseball caps, rap music, and so on.

However, conceptualizing globalization as nothing but Americanization or Westernization is unrealistic and perhaps simplistic. A fundamental concern of globalization is power; its instrumentalities and how they are variously organized, manifested, expressed, and exercised (Held and McGrew 2002, p. 8). Foucault (1994b) presents a version of power that reflects the realities of globalization. Though globalization demonstrates the geopolitical, geocultural, and international power relations between the United States, the world's sole superpower, and the rest of the world, globalization does not involve the complete global domination of one culture or technology over others. According to Michel Foucault (1994a),

> political power has deeper roots than is suspected. It is diffuse and operates through invisible, little-known centers and fulcrums. Even institutions that seem to be neutral and independent are instruments of political power. However, power is not only oppressive, it is also productive. It produces knowledge and discourse that constructs the reality of the world to the exclusion of other realities.

Foucault suggests that no nation willfully and deliberately strives for a type of global domination that "reverberates from top to bottom" (p. 181). Indeed, rather than being a top-down, center-to-periphery affair, power exists at all levels. "The important thing is to analyze how, at the most elemental level, procedures of power spread and are modified; how they are invested and annexed by global phenomena and how technologies and economic profits come into play in the game of power relations" (Foucault 1994b). The structural adjustment programs and technology transfer projects negotiated between the international community (led by the World Bank and the International Monetary Fund) and poor Third World countries reflect asymmetrical power dynamics. Telecommunications and government policies almost always flow from powerful nations and centers of power to developing and transitioning countries and regions of the world through supranational organizations, individual nation-states, and governmental and nongovernmental organizations.

However, power, which always has technological and economic dimensions, is invested and annexed by global phenomena at the most elemental level of the world order. Thus, all nations actively or passively play a role in the global, high-stakes distribution of power. Therefore, globalization is not the global domination by one culture or technology over all other cultures and technologies. Globalization is the result of how technology, economics, and communications enter into the game of power relations, in which all countries and cultures are players (Foucault 1994b). This is consonant with the concept of hegemony.

Hegemony has been described as a consensual political and cultural relationship between a dominant class or culture and subaltern, or subordinate, cultures or social groups, in which the latter are subject to the initiatives and interests of the former. Since the subordinate class or culture gives its active consent to the relationship—for reasons of cultural prestige—the roles of either party are not usually viewed as coercive or submissive (Gramsci 1996, p. 21, p. 91). Indeed, if people from the subaltern culture consume products from the dominant culture, especially if it is from another country or region of the world, they can be said to "undergo the moral and intellectual hegemony of foreign intellectuals" (Gramsci 1996, p. 63).

Hegemony is usually a negotiated process that almost always involves power and a purpose. Rich, dominant political and cultural entities subtly and even unconsciously provide new values, worldviews, and meanings that affect and transform poorer countries at a psychological and cognitive level (Gramsci 1985). This occurs because the culture-industries and governments of rich countries provide, with the consent of poorer countries, entertaining programming that the audiences of poorer countries enjoy.

In Africa, television programming is obtained through direct acquisition of cheap American reruns and movies from international television program markets. Programming is also obtained free of any charge from the international communication arms of the United States, Britain,

France, Germany, and other governments, as part of bilateral agreements. French hegemony continues in the French-speaking post-colonies of Africa through negotiated cooperation agreements under the auspices of the French government–funded Organisation Internationale de la Francophonie (International Organization of French-Speaking Countries), whose main aim is the promotion of French language and culture (Eko 2003b). As part of the Francophonie system, the French government provides French-speaking African countries with programming from the French government broadcaster, Canal France International (French International Channel), and TV5. In order to increase French-language content on the Internet, La Francophonie trains computer, Internet technicians, and content producers in the latest Web page development, e-commerce, and other online activities.

AFRICAN MEDIA DEREGULATION, GLOBALIZATION, AND COMMERCIALIZATION

Many African countries were sucked into the vortex of globalization against their wish. The fall of the Berlin Wall in 1989 and the end of the Cold War triggered a fierce hurricane of instability and popular uprisings across sub-Saharan Africa (Monga 1996: Eko 2003b; Eko 2003c). Opposition parties were legalized and press laws were liberalized as well. The major international financial institutions, namely the World Bank and the International Monetary Fund, imposed a series of conditions on African governmental borrowers: structural adjustment, deregulation, privatization, and commercialization of governmental corporations in telecommunications, broadcasting, and other sectors (Van Audenhove et al. 2001; Ihonvbere and Mbaku 2003). Additionally, the IMF and the World Bank imposed "universal patterns of political and financial integrity" (Nelken 2003, pp. 437–458). These powerful international forces dramatically transformed the media situation in Africa.

That was the thin edge of the wedge of globalization. Indeed, the work of the United Nations and other international organizations in setting standards in the developing and transitional countries of the world for human rights, good governance, transparency and accountability in financial management, institution building, and harmony and uniformity in international trade law, among other activities, is aimed at creating a seamless, American-style, global, electronic economy marked by a fluid exchange of goods, services, information, intellectual property products, and capital (Eko 2001; Monge and Contractor 2003, p. 142). These policies essentially globalized America's capitalist, neoliberal free-market values (Monge and Contractor 2003, p. 142). Additionally, the policies of the G7, the world's most industrialized countries, toward Africa were driven by a concern for liberalized markets, increased competition, and access to African networks (Van Audenhove et al. 2001).

Many poor African countries signed on to these IMF and World Bank rules, which essentially transfer neoliberal, open-market policies to their countries, in order to obtain concessionary loans or merely to postpone the day of reckoning with international bankers and these same lending institutions. The results of these programs are evident in telecommunications and broadcasting on the African continent. Dozens of private, African-owned radio stations (legal and pirate) have appeared, like noisy colonies of weaver birds in the African forests. Virtually all African countries now have a multitude of private radio and television stations broadcasting side by side the government stations. This new group of broadcasters is a mixed bag of private, commercial, and community broadcasters. In many cases, governmental broadcasters have commercialized their programming in a bid to shore up their dwindling funds, obtain cheap programming, and hold on to their audiences (Eko 2003c). These governmental broadcasters have had to quickly transition from broadcasters who operated without regard to ratings and audience research to competitive, mixed-economy corporations that were still mandated to promote nation-building and national unity, as well as to continue development communication, in a changing legal, increasingly globalized, market-oriented environment. Many abandoned relatively expensive productions and opted for cheap or free programs from international broadcasters. Most started FM stations that broadcast American-style Top 40 commercial music programming. The result is the homogenization of programming. Public broadcast stations are beginning to sound like their private commercial counterparts.

As African public broadcasters try to reinvent themselves to adapt to the new environment of globalization and market competition, we now have a situation where, in the view of Mattelart (2002), the freedom of commercial communication takes precedence over the rights of citizens to free, democratic speech. Indeed, Africa is the new frontier of advertising. Advertising has become ubiquitous. From Addis Ababa, Ethiopia, to Zomba, Malawi, from Senegal to Djibouti, and from Egypt to South Africa, advertising rules. Giant billboards, radio jingles, television commercials, and mobile cinema vans exhort Africans to buy and consume all kinds of goods that promise so-called Westernization: beauty, happiness, health, satisfaction, youthfulness, success, and wealth. On radio and television, advertising messages have drowned out the once-popular developmental and cultural programming.

Indeed, global advertising has taken Africa by storm. The bulk of continent-wide or regional advertising is produced in Europe by multinational corporations marketing products ranging from European and African beers to American and British cigarettes, from cellular phone services to Asian-made condoms. In Cameroon, two of the most popular advertising slogans are "Guinness Is Good for You," an ad for the Irish brewery, Arthur Guinness and Sons, and *"33 Export, la Blonde des Blondes"* ("33 Export, the Blonde of Blondes"), an ad for a locally produced version of a French beer that is popular in francophone Africa. Africa No.1, the continent's first transnational French-language commercial station, advertises Mercedes Benz trucks as "The Elephant of the African Road," while the Marlboro Man invites Africans to "Come to Marlboro Country" in gravelly, Parisian-accented intonations. British cigarette manufacturer Benson and Hedges invites Africans to "Discover Gold, Discover Benson and Hedges." The list of ads goes on and on. Africa is in the vortex of global advertising. That has not always been the case. Indeed, Africa is one of the last places on earth where tobacco is still advertised on radio, television, and billboards. Efforts to curtail tobacco advertising and tobacco promotion in Africa and other developing regions of the world have been undermined or blocked by the Anglo-American tobacco industry (Moulson 2000).

When African nations became self-governing in the late 1950s and early 1960s, most of them inherited the media setups of the former colonial administrations. Post-independence media in Africa was thus a mishmash of imitations of European models. Broadcasting stations in the former British colonies of East, Central, Southern, and West Africa were funded by a mixture of one-time radio and television licenses (often paid at the time a set was purchased), meager advertising, and government subsidies. Indeed, these systems were described as a "brood of more or less dutiful offspring" of the BBC (Ainslie 1966, p. 158).

Media systems in francophone countries were politicized government bureaucracies funded in whole by the government. What little advertising they received was often channeled to the stations through a government-owned advertising agency. That was the situation until globalization and commercialization reached African shores in the wake of the fall of the Berlin Wall in 1989.

As advertising became the norm in African broadcasting, a subtle note of resistance against commercialization was heard on the radio from time to time. In the middle of a French-style advertising break on the national network of Radio Cameroon, advertisements for European products faded smoothly into a heavily accented African voice that intoned, rather jocularly, "Suabva-Makabva, the natural palm wine that neutralizes the tropical heat! Suabva-Makabva, the drink whose cool freshness eliminates the sweat of Africa! Drink Suabva-Makabva!" The thirty-second African ad sandwiched between slick foreign-produced ads became a favorite of listeners. The problem with this ad was that it was a parody of advertising. Suabva-Makabva was a fictitious drink! The fake ad had been recorded and cleverly edited into the tape of the station's paid advertisements. When the parody was discovered, the managers of the station, who had gotten used to hearing the funny ad, were not amused! They promptly removed it from the advertising lineup.

INTERNATIONAL AND SURROGATE BROADCASTING, POWER, AND HEGEMONY

Since the IMF and World Bank–driven "liberalization" got underway in Africa, several major international broadcasters who used to broadcast only on shortwave radio to Africa, have entered into agreements with African governments to broadcast directly to African audiences on the FM band. Indeed, in many African countries, it is easier, for political reasons for international broadcasters to obtain broadcast licenses than it is for Africans.

The changing political fortunes of the Ivory Coast demonstrate the nature of broadcast surrogacy in Africa. In 2004, aircraft from the French military base in Abidjan, Port Bouet, Ivory Coast, attacked and destroyed all the aircraft of their former colony, the war-torn Ivory Coast, and seized the country's main airport in Abidjan. The attack was retaliation for an Ivorian army air raid against rebel positions that ended up killing eight members of a French peacekeeping contingent in the front lines of the conflict. When anti-French riots broke out in the streets of Abidjan, the economic capital of the Ivory Coast, the French army was sent to evacuate French citizens. A confrontation with demonstrators led to the shooting of tens of civilians. The government of the Ivory Coast promptly closed down the *Radio France Internationale* (RFI) FM station in Abidjan, where thousands of French citizens lived. *Radio France Internationale*, Paris, ultimately sent evacuation instructions through shortwave radio broadcasts and the Internet. The closure of RFI Abidjan FM was a temporary setback in the French government's policy of starting FM stations in Africa to broadcast or rebroadcast RFI's programming to the African continent.

French international broadcast policies in Africa reflect the intense competition between the world's leading international broadcasters over the airwaves, and specifically, the Frequency Modulation (FM) band on the African continent. *Radio France Internationale* is involved in a fierce struggle with Voice of America (VOA), the British Broadcasting Corporation (BBC), *Radio Deutsche Welle* (Voice of Germany), *Radio Television Portuguès Internacional*, and others, to use FM stations in Africa to distribute programming originating from their home countries. By 2003, Voice of America had a network of over fourteen hundred surrogate radio and television affiliates in forty-four countries across the linguistic zones of Africa (VOA 2005). France had sixty-five FM stations in thirty-three African countries, while the BBC had thirty-two FM stations in fourteen countries.

The VOA's foray into Africa is part of its Radio Democracy for Africa project, aimed at creating surrogate, or affiliate, radio operations throughout Africa to promote democracy. In order to expand this effort, the U.S. House of Representatives passed the *Promoting Independent Broadcasting in Africa Act* (U.S. Congress 1998). The bill, based on the premise that promotion of independent radio in Africa is a useful tool for advancing democracy and human rights, provides VOA's African affiliates with the means to relay or rebroadcast American programming. The United States is undoubtedly the dominant international broadcaster on the African airwaves. Indeed, in 2004, Voice of America television programs were transmitted live or recorded and retransmitted in thirty-two television stations in fourteen African countries.

The process of surrogate broadcasting in Africa is a textbook example of power dynamics, influence, and hegemony. In order to become an affiliate of Voice of America, licensed governmental, nongovernmental, and private stations sign agreements outlining the contours of "cooperation" between VOA and the prospective affiliates. The letter of agreement stipulates VOA's commitment to supply programming by satellite, the Internet, or other means. It also outlines the prospective affiliate's agreement to broadcast certain Voice of America programs at certain times, for specific periods (VOA 2005). VOA has signed a series of affiliate agreements with governmental departments, ministries, broadcasting organizations, as well as with community and private African radio stations.

The French governmental international broadcaster, RFI, has also entered into a series of bilateral agreements with governmental and private sector broadcasters across Africa. These agreements give the French flagbearer unprecedented access to African airwaves and audiences. The BBC has, with the backing of the British government, also leveraged its international reputation and influence in Africa into a series of agreements with African governments that have given the international broadcaster licenses to operate FM stations in Africa. These stations relay and rebroadcast programs produced in London. BBC African stations broadcast in English, French, Swahili, and tens of other African languages. Thus, the BBC competes directly with African governmental and private radio stations, as well as against French, American, Portuguese, German, and other broadcasters. Indeed, in order to give an African flavor to its broadcasts, the BBC has taken on a whole new look and feel in Africa. The

BBC's thirty-two FM stations on the African continent—and they range from BBC Antananarivo, Madagascar, 89.2 FM to BBC Zanzibar, Tanzania, 94.1 FM—all have an exotic ring to them. However, the programming broadcast over these stations is classic BBC World Service fare. All broadcasts originate from London and are produced from an unmistakable British perspective. There is very little or no local content in the broadcasts. The same is true for VOA, RFI, Radio Deutsch Welle, and others.

Ironically, most Africans who apply for FM broadcast licenses are denied for political, financial, and other reasons. The only major African broadcast organization that features in this competition is the Pan-African, French-language commercial station, Africa No. 1, which has FM stations in a number of African capitals and in Paris, France (Eko 2004c).

At face value, the picture of international surrogate broadcasting in Africa looks like the picture of postcolonial domination and cultural imperialism. Nevertheless, the deployment of international power and influence on the African airwaves was done with the active participation and agreement of Africans. All stations were started after bilateral talks and diplomatic agreements between African governments and these international broadcasters or their governments (Enogo 2001). Many African countries signed on to these hegemonic relationships for political, economic, or cultural reasons. The result is a replication of postcolonial relationships of dependence and subordination across the linguistic zones of Africa.

The contemporary international broadcast scene in Africa is an interesting reflection of global power dynamics and Western hegemony. Indeed, by its very nature, international communication is an act of power that reproduces asymmetrical power relations between rich and poor, former colonizer and former colony (Mbembe 2001). Michel Foucault advanced the view that communication is power; communication always has elements of power relations since to communicate is to act on the other. Indeed, news discourse is an element in the strategic deployment of power-relations apparatus. Foucault (1994b) advanced a succinct description of media products as instruments of power relations:

> power relations are exercised most importantly, through the production and exchange of signs. . . . The production and dissemination of media messages has power consequences. As for communication involving finished [media] products . . . the very fact that they change the informative sphere of the participants, has power effects . . . power relations are expressed through the production and dissemination of signs and finished media products. (p. 234)

Additionally, the selection of international news and programming content is an act of discursive power. Using Derrida's concept of communicative "re-presentation" (1967), Legrand suggests that re-presentation, or the act of presenting texts anew, takes place in the context of unequal power relations between a *re-presenter* (the self) and a *re-presented* (the other): "The choice of material by the re-presenter is an act of power. . . . the act of selection, therefore, insensibly moves the selector from the descriptive to the prescriptive mode. . . . Because it is never strictly constative (or iconic), description is ascription" (2003, p. 254).

MEDIA LIBERALIZATION AND THE SATIRICAL PRESS

One of the hallmarks of the post–Cold War liberalization of the African media was the emergence of a new breed of journalism in sub-Saharan Africa: the caustic, irreverent, satirical press (Eko 2003b). Indeed, political cartoons became symbols of democratization and liberalization (Waltremez 1992; Mason 2001). The African satirical press reflects global influences. It is a mélange of indigenous satirical art and European comic journalism. Indeed, the satirical press of francophone West and Central Africa has been influenced by the French satirical journalism that came to the continent through the forces of colonialism, globalization, and partnerships between some French satirical newspapers, like *Le Canard Enchainé*, and African satirical newspapers (Waltremez 1992). Drawing upon the continent's many artistic traditions and visual cultures—from highly expressive masks to abstract expressionistic totemic art—African caricaturists, cartoonists, and comic strip artists use humor and satire to expose the contradictions, hypocrisies, and abuses of power of the continent's elite. They have brought ridicule and contempt on the greedy and corrupt political and military elites, and their neocolonial European partners. They are thus the public whipping posts of the rich and powerful, as well as the "forces of law and disorder" (Waltremez 1992). The following section will focus on four satirical publications that are representative of the African satirical press of the post–Cold War era: *Le Cafard Libéré*, *Le Marabout*, *Le Messager Popoli*, and *Le Gri Gri International*. These newspapers are mostly written in a hodgepodge of French and African lingua franca like Wolof, Moré, and pidgin English.

Le Cafard Libéré

Le Cafard Libéré of Dakar, Senegal, was one of the first satirical newspapers to sprout on the African continent in the post–Cold War years. Senegal has one of Africa's most stable multiparty democracies. It has not had any coups d'état though it has a simmering, low-level separatist insurgency in its Casamance region. Senegal has one of the most vibrant press traditions in Africa.

Corruption is part of the tableau of African politics. (Cartoon by Kiendsongda Oué-draogo [Songda] of *Le Marabout*, Ouagadougou, Burkina Faso.)

Le Marabout

Le Marabout—a play on the word *Marabout*, which means *Marabou* (the bird) in French, and *soothsayer*, or *traditional healer*, in several West African languages—is published by the African Network for Freedom of Information (RALI). It combines well-written satirical and opinion pieces with high-quality artistic cartoons. Its two cartoonists, award-winning Kiend-songda Ouédraogo (Songda) and Damien Glez (who also doubles as the editor-in-chief), raked African politicians and their international partners over the coals. Unfortunately, like many upstart, post–Cold War African newspapers, the print version of *Le Marabout* folded after two years of publication, for lack of adequate advertising revenue. In effect, in Burkina Faso as in most African countries, powerful politicians who are the subjects of satire pressurize advertisers to boycott critical newspapers. Many fold as a result. Today, *Le Marabout* publishes only an online version.

Le Gri Gri International

Le Gri Gri International of Libreville, Gabon, is a "replacement" newspaper. It was created by a group of journalists and caricaturists whose acerbic, pun-filled, satirical former newspaper, *La Griffe* (*The Claw*), had been banned by the authoritarian government of Omar Bongo, a staunch French ally who has been in power in Gabon for more than thirty-five years. The history of journalism in Gabon shows that, despite post–Cold War liberalization, being a cartoonist, caricaturist, or a satirical comic strip artist in Africa is not without its risks.

In February of 2002, Michel Ongoundou Loundah, editor of *La Griffe* (*The Claw*), an irreverent newspaper also based in Libreville, Gabon, survived a kidnapping and murder attempt. He fled to neighboring Cameroon where he sought political refuge. This was the culmination of a tumultuous year in which Loundah's much censored, often-seized newspaper was banned indefinitely and its whole editorial staff barred from practicing journalism in Gabon. The government banned the newspaper and its "replacement," *Le Gri Gri International*, for publishing articles and cartoons "bordering on provocation against the head of state" (Reporters Without Borders 2002). In effect, some cartoons and articles in the newspaper had reported that the president's daughter, who was a member of his cabinet, was involved in a ritual murder for hire.

In addition to the ban, the whole editorial staff of the newspaper was barred from practicing journalism in Gabon indefinitely. Ongoudou relaunched the "replacement" newspaper *Le Gri-Gri International* (*International Gri Gri*) from France where he promptly reported that his newspaper *La Griffe* was the "victim of a fatwa" (Islamic edict) from Mollah Omar B. This was a play on the name of President Omar Bongo of Gabon, and the name of the leader of the Taliban, Mullah Omar. Even before the ban, the government had pressured advertisers in *La Griffe* and *Le Gri Gri International*, forcing them to stop advertising in the newspapers. *Le Gri Gri International* now publishes both a hard copy and an online version from France.

"African scene on the banks of the Seine": Leaders of French-speaking African countries dancing to the neocolonial tune of French president Jacques Chirac. (Cartoon by Nyemb Popoli, *Le Messager Popoli*, Nov. 26, 1998.)

Le Messager Popoli

Le Messager Popoli is based in Douala, Cameroon. The country can best be described as a semi-authoritarian regime. Le Messager Group, which owned *Le Messager Popoli* until it was divested, has made a name for itself as one of the most indefatigable defenders of freedom of conscience and of the press in Africa (Eko 2003a). *Le Messager Popoli* was launched in the heyday of post–Cold War democratization. Its very survival is a record. The newspaper has been censored, its journalists and cartoonists harassed and imprisoned. On its tenth anniversary in 2002, one of the newspaper's cartoonists, El Pacho (2002), who uses only his nom de plume, described the newspaper's ten-year existence as one that was "dominated by tempests of censorship, storms of death threats, winds of abductions, cyclones of forced exile and playing hide and seek" with law enforcement officials (p. 3).

Despite these negative experiences, the African satirical press has carved out a niche for itself on the media landscape. Visual satire, an African tradition that was stifled during the colonial period and the one-party Cold War era, is now an indispensable part of African journalism (Eko 2005). African cartoons will continue to be instruments for the demystification and demythification of Africa's "republican monarchs" and military strongmen. The press in Africa reflects the uneasy power relations between the government and civil society. Indeed, the satirical press

Lessons from the IMF to African presidents, the ABCs of structural adjustment: "Globalize your economy, privatize, import. . . . Localize your poverty, immigration, AIDS, Ebola . . ." (Cartoon by Nyemb Popoli, *Le Messager Popoli,* July 1999.)

has in its own way served as a counter-power to the political authorities. Despite heavy-handed attempts in some countries to crush it, the African satirical press gets stronger when it confronts abuse of power.

BRIDGING THE DIGITAL DIVIDE THROUGH REINVENTION OF THE INTERNET

World system theory holds that the world is divided between the core and the periphery, the North and the South, the rich and the poor (Held and McGrew 2002, p. 77). These structural inequalities are the result of historical phenomena such as slavery and colonialism, as well as postcolonial economic exploitation (Mattelart 2002). Furthermore, technological developments have transformed the world into a networked society in which the informational paradigm of knowledge creation, economic productivity, and the fluid flow of information and financial capital across geographic regions and national territories has transformed Northern economies in the post–Cold War era (Castells 2000, p. 20). This globalization of the world's economy has further exacerbated the structural fragmentation of the world into winners and losers, leading to the rise of fundamentalism, terrorism, ethnic, religious, and other conflicts (Castells 2000; Mattellart 2002; Mittelman 2004).

The disparities between North and South are reflected in a wide array of indicators, ranging from income levels to access to information and communication technologies. One of the most obvious manifestations of the structural division of the world is the global divide (Slouka 1995). The global divide is presented as the differential access to the Internet and other information and communication technologies found between the industrialized countries of the North and the developing countries of the South, as well as the consequences of these differences for global economic development. One of the structural problems in Africa is the lack of basic communication facilities. This has essentially consigned the African continent to the margins of the global economy (Opoku-Mensah 2001). Indeed, since the 1990s, the official UN technology and connectivity policy toward Africa has been the "leapfrogging" approach, which holds that information and communication technologies would enable Africa to skip several stages in the development process and reduce the digital divide between the continent and the rest of the world (Eko 2004a). This policy was based on the ideology of information technology, which assumes a causal link between increased productivity, economic growth, and information technology (Burnett and Marshall 2003).

Africa's position in the global communications system changed dramatically in 2001 when a $700 million, 28,000 kilometer (17,500 mile) underwater fiber-optic cable system, SAT-3/WASC (South Africa/West Africa to Europe) and SAFE (South Africa to the Far East) was inaugurated. The project successfully linked the African continent to the major telecommunications hubs of Europe, North America, the Middle East, and Asia. The system, which was designed to serve African telecommunication needs for twenty-five years, was the most significant telecommunications achievement in African history. When it was first commissioned, it directly linked ten African countries to global telecommunications hubs. A further twenty-six landlocked African countries were scheduled to be connected to the system (SAT-3/WASC/SAFE 2004). The connection resulted in a dramatic change in telecommunications capacity in general, and Internet connectivity in particular, on a continent that had been relegated to the periphery of global telecommunications for decades (Ndao 2003; Eko 2004; Jensen 2001).

However, mere connectivity did not resolve Africa's communication and economic problems. Indeed, the contrary was true. The fiber-optic project created a bigger pipeline for the flow of global Internet content to the African continent. The project effectively made the African continent part of the market-based, laissez-faire, neoliberal, e-commerce regime advanced by the Clinton administration (Clinton and Gore 1997) and confirmed by the Supreme Court of the United States (*Reno* v. *ACLU* 1997).

In a series on Internet connectivity in Africa, *Boston Globe* reporter Hiawatha Bray noted that bringing Africa into the globalized electronic economy would be a slow process because outside South Africa there were fewer than a million credit cards in circulation on the entire continent (2001a). The reporter featured an African Internet visionary and entrepreneur who was launching E-Touch debit cards on the continent with the hope of convincing Africans to "embrace the plastic-based (electronic) economy" (2001b). For her part, former Hewlett–Packard CEO Carly Fiorina was quoted as saying that Africa would be the next growth market for high technology. As a result, her company was targeting its world E-Inclusion program to the four billion people worldwide who were and are ignored by traditional information technology companies (Bray 2001a).

Indeed, the global economy reached the most inaccessible place on the African continent—Timbuktu, Mali—thanks to the efforts of the American government. The "new" competitive global market economy was introduced to the nomads, artisans, and craftsmen and women of Timbuktu by the American experts, who brought Internet telecommunication technology to the sandstorm capital of the world. The Americans, working under the auspices of a U.S. Agency for International Development (U.S. AID) project called the Africa Global Information Infrastructure Project (Leyland Initiative), established satellite links and proceeded to create Web pages advertising local products and services from the outside world, amid the burning sun, sandstorms, and abject poverty of the Sahara Desert (Barlow 1999). The Internet also came to tens of other African towns and villages under the Leyland Initiative (U.S. AID 1999).

The Leyland Initiative and the African underwater fiber-optic project accelerated the delivery of Western content to the African continent without any consideration of cultural relevance and acceptability. Additionally, connectivity took place in the absence of Internet regulatory frameworks. In short, connectivity projects have accelerated the transfer of what Nelken calls the Western culture of "expressive individualism" to Africa, a continent with a decidedly communitarian ethic (2003, p. 45). Additionally, the information and communication technologies, as well as the content that Africans have suddenly been granted access to, are subject to Western legal and commercial imperatives (Ngenda 2005). Such communication ignores local African cultures, knowledge, and competencies. Emphasis on connectivity and access for their own sake essentially leave the accessing countries of Africa at the mercy of the cultures, values, and ideals of the dominant regulators, software writers, hardware manufacturers, and content producers of the industrialized countries.

From a cultural perspective, the most important component of Internet and information and communication technologies is probably the architecture or 'code' of the technologies. Indeed, through code, information and communication technologies are used to regulate the behavior of users on a global scale, in accordance with the values, ideals, and ethics of the manufacturers, controllers, and hardware and software designers (Shah and Kesan 2003).

Indeed, American and European policymakers and regulators "are using or advocating architectural solutions to address societal concerns with crime, competition, security, free speech, privacy, the protection of intellectual property, and revitalizing democratic discourse" (Shah and Kesan 2003, p. 3). Most of these problems are specific to the Western world. The implication is that policymakers and software designers are essentially manipulating and regulating behavior, such as the preservation of anonymity or the tracking of Internet users on a global scale, through the architecture of the information and communication technologies. Shah and Kesan highlight the "power of code" as a regulatory mechanism for filtering Internet content through viewpoint-independent or content-based labeling systems that monitor Web users through the insertion of cookies, protection or infringement of individual privacy, promotion or stifling of innovation, and protection or infringement of intellectual property through default and standard settings (2003, p. 5). Furthermore, the design of Internet architecture is an entry barrier against powerless end users from the Third World, especially those who speak languages other than English or French. This essentially results in what African philosopher

Hountondji calls Africa's "dispersion in the global," with the active consent of the continent's political elite (2000 p. 47). This is the very essence of hegemony borne of asymmetric power relations.

In answer to these cultural challenges posed by the globalization of the Internet, some African computer scientists, linguists, and academics have embarked on the slow process of reinventing, Africanizing, and localizing some information and communication technologies. This is done through the gradual process of producing content in African languages, using African scripts, if necessary, and making such content available to Africans who do not speak English or French, do not have electricity, and cannot afford computers. Africa is a continent that has hundreds of languages. Only a few of these are spoken by more than one million people. The major computer and software companies do not, therefore, find these languages commercially viable. Indeed, Microsoft has written Windows XP and Windows 2003 in only two African languages, Afrikaans and Swahili. Though Swahili is now the official language of the African Union, the cost of software in that language is prohibitive. That leaves millions of Africans with Internet content, when it is available, only in foreign languages.

AFRICAN REINVENTION OF THE INTERNET

The first and most successful translation of information and communication technologies into an African language was carried out by expatriate Ethiopians. As early as the 1980s, these computer and electrical engineers who were studying and working in the United States, Canada, and Europe, individually, and at their own expense, translated the ancient Ethiopian glyphic script, Ge'ez, into computer code and fonts. The Ethiopic script became available for personal computers before many European languages. These engineers also developed keyboards and software for DOS, Windows, and Mac. The Dashen Ethiopic word processor has been on the market since 1985. It effectively brought the eighty-seven Ethiopic and Eritrean languages into the digital age. Today, Microsoft Word, Word Perfect, and other popular software packages have been translated into Ethiopic. This has enabled Web page development and Internet access in Amharic and other Ethiopic languages for millions of Ethiopians and Eritreans around the world. Unfortunately, the U.S. AID's Leyland Initiative in Ethiopia was solely in English. Ethiopian and other African developers are standardizing their products and trying to influence hardware and software makers to incorporate Ethiopic, Yoruba, Hausa, Xhosa, Shona, Zula, and others as standard languages in computing.

A notable localization of information and communication technologies into an African language through translation of computer code is taking place at the University of Dar es Salaam in Tanzania. The Open Swahili Localization Project of the Department of Computer Science, working in collaboration with a Swedish IT consultancy company, has used Linux to write a lot of software in Swahili that can be downloaded free of charge (Eko 2004a). This includes the Win32 version of JamboOpenOffice. The project is currently working on the first-ever Swahili open-source Web browser, Firefox 1.01.

Linux-based OpenOffice has also been translated into Afrikaans, Sepedi, Venda, and Zulu (Marson 2004). This mostly volunteer project was funded in part by the South African government and private foundations. Additionally, the Mozilla Web browser has been translated into Xhosa. It runs on Windows, Linux, and Mac. In response to the massive and successful volunteer translation of open source software into several African languages, Microsoft's Local Language Program indicated that the company was willing to collaborate with third parties to distribute Language Interface Packs as a localization solution for "emerging language" markets (Marson 2004). This is clearly a response to African attempts to produce content in African languages. The result is that, starting with newspapers, more and more African online content will be available in various African languages. The genius of the Internet—its decentralization, openness, redundancy, simplicity, ubiquity, and statelessness—lend themselves to innovation even in circumstances of hegemony and asymmetrical power relations as in sub-Saharan Africa. Africans have shown they can bridge the digital divide through localization and domestication of the Internet.

THE GLOBALIZATION OF HEGEMONY

Post–Cold War liberalization and globalization led to increased Western involvement in broadcasting on the African continent (Eko 2003c). Crisp, clear, digital voices from outside of Africa—mostly from the United States, Great Britain, France, Germany, Portugal, and Arabia—now rise above the traditional, exotic gumbo of languages that has been the hallmark of the African airwaves. The International Monetary Fund and the World Bank have universalized neoliberal economics, promoted a global free-market system, and reshaped the economies, telecommunications policies, and institutions of tens of developing countries (Mittelman 2004).

From the perspective of hegemony, institutions like the IMF and the World Bank, which appear to be neutral and independent in their advocacy of deregulation, privatization, and other market solutions, are indeed instruments of political power. The structural adjustment programs of the IMF and the World Bank have changed life on the African continent in negative ways, exacerbating unequal power relations and dynamics through political and economic cooperation between nation-states and private transnational corporations, foreign assistance and development aid for privatization, and loans from developed countries to developing countries. Furthermore, the United Nations, through its communications activities, as well as those of its specialized agencies, has been one of the main agents of policy transfer and globalization. Additionally, although official UN policy champions the globalization of human rights, including freedom of speech and of the press, the realization of these policies and rights are elusive.

Significantly, telecommunications policy transfers, structural adjustment programs, privatization, and commercialization are carried out with the active consent and participation of the African countries concerned. Indeed, hegemony is part of a package negotiated by Africa's political and cultural elite on behalf of their nations, largely at the expense of democracy and the interests of the majority—an expense that includes a lack of access to the production and distribution of media by the working classes, peasants, and poor. Globalization and hegemony consign Africa, through the continent's "dispersal in the universal" (Hountondji 2000) to what Mbembe calls "an unreality of powerlessness" (2001, p. 4). Nonetheless, some Africans are using information and communications technologies to resist homegrown tyrants and the cultural homogeneity of globalization.

APPENDIX: LIST OF MAJOR MEDIA IN AFRICA BY COUNTRY

Television

Angola
Televisão de Angola
Benin
La Chaine 2 International (contact)
Benin TV
Botswana
GBC TV 23
Burkina Faso
Burkina Faso Television (website)
Burundi
Burundi National Radio and Television
Cameroon
CRTV Cameroon
Central African Republic
Central African Republic Communications
Congo (Kinshasa)
RTNC Bandundu
Antenne A
Canal Tropical Television Tropicana TV (contact)
Canal Z
CMB TV
Radio Television Nationale Congolaise (RTNC1)
RTNC2 Kinshasa
Raga TV
RTGA
Horizon 33
TKM
CCTV

CKTV
Digital Congo
Global TV
Côte d'Ivoire
TVCI Ivory Coast
Abidjan
Radio Télévision Ivoirienne
Djibouti
Djibouti Radio and TV
Radiodiffusion Television de Djibouti
Ethiopia
Ethiopian Television
GHMC
Gabon
Telediffusions Gabonaises
Ghana
Christian Entertainment TV
GTV (Ghana)
Metropolitan Entertainment TV
TV Africa
TV3
Ghana Broadcasting Corporation
  (website, contact)
Media TV
Guinea
Guinea Radio-Television (RTG)
Kenya
EATV 37
EATV 30
EATV 53
Kenya Broadcasting Company
East Africa TV (EATV)
EATV 43
Lesotho
LTV 29
Malawi
Malawi Broadcasting Corporation
Mali
Télévision Nationale—Bamako
Office de Radiodiffusion Television du
  Mali (ORTM)
Mauritius
Mauritius Broadcasting Corporation
Morocco
Radiodiffusion Television Marocaine
Mozambique
STV 37

STV 29
Televisão de Moçambique
Namibia
Namibian Broadcasting Corporation
Niger
Niger Radio and Television
Nigeria
PRTV Corporation
NTA Jos
DBN International (website)
Nigerian Television Authority
TV 39
Silverbird TV (website)
Channels Television (website)
Africa Independent Television (web-
  site)
MITV
Senegal
RACECO Group
ORTS Senegal
Seychelles
Seychelles Broadcasting Corporation
South Africa
South African Broadcasting Corpora-
tion
E-TV
Extreme Sports Channel
Uplink TV
M-Net
Deukom Group
Swaziland
Swazi TV
Tanzania
Independent Television Ltd (ITV)
DTV 40
East Africa Television (EATV)
Televisheni ya Taifa (TVT)
TV Zanzibar
Togo
Television Togolaise
Uganda
International Television Network Ltd
International TV Network Uganda
TV Africa 28
East Africa Television (EATV)
Zambia
TV Africa 8

Zambia National Broadcasting Corporation
TV Africa 21
Zimbabwe
Zimbabwe Broadcasting Corporation

Radio

Algeria
Algerian Radio
Angola
Radio Angola
Channel Africa
Radio Ecclesia
Benin
Radio France Internationale
Africa No. 1
Golfe FM
Burkina Faso
Radio France Internationale
Africa No. 1
Radio Pulsar
Burundi
Radio France Internationale
Cameroon
CRTV
Cape Verde
Cabonet
Central African Republic
Africa No.1
Chad
Africa No. 1
Côte d'Ivoire
Radiodiffusion Television Ivoirienne
Africa No. 1
Radio France Internationale
Nostalgie
Democratic Republic of Congo
Blue Sky Radio
Equatorial Guinea
Radio Africa
Egypt
Arab Radio and Television Network
Visafric
Arab Radio
Egypt Radio Amateurs Assembly

Eritrea
Meskerem
The Eritrean Political Opposition-
Visafric
Ethiopia
The Voice of Ethiopian Medhin
The Voice of Ethiopian Unity
Radio Ethiopia
Voice of Oromo Liberation (OLF)
Equatorial Guinea
Radio Africa
Gabon
Africa No. 1
Ghana
Choice 102.3FM
Ghana Broadcasting Corporation
Vibe FM
Guinea Bissau
Channel Africa
Kenya
Capital FM
East FM
Liberia
Blue Sky Radio
Liberia Communication Network
Madagascar
Radio Madagasikara
Radio France Internationale
Mali
Radio Canal
Radio France Internationale
Radio Douentza
Impact Data
Africa No. 1
Mauritius
Mauritius Broadcasting
Morocco
Radio Casablanca
Radio Mediterranee
Mozambique
Macua de Moçambique
Channel Africa
Namibia
Namibian Broadcasting
Association
Niger
Africa No. 1

Nigeria
National Broadcasting Commission
Cool FM
Voice of Odudwa, Radio Yoruba
National Association of Yoruba Descendants in North America
Reunion
Eccueil
Reseau France Outre-Mer
Sao Tome
Channel Africa
Senegal
Nostalgie
Seychelles
Far East Broadcasting Association
Somalia
Radio Somalialand
RSL Somaliland Independent Radio
South Africa
SAFMSouth African Radio
Radio Algoa
5FM
Impact Radio
Punt
Afrikaans Talk Radio
RMR
Rhodes Music Radio (student-run radio station of Rhodes University)
Sudan
Sudan Radio
Voice of Sudan
St. Helena
Radio St. Helena
Swaziland
Gospel Radio

Tanzania
Radio One
Tunisia
Radio Tunisia
Uganda
Radio France Internationale
Zimbabwe
Zimbabwe Broadcasting Corporation
ZBC 1, ZBC 2, ZBC 3, ZBC 4

Newspapers (partial list of major papers)

Daily Nation (Kenya)
www.nationmedia.com/dailynation/
The East African (Kenya)
www.nationmedia.com/eastafrican/current/
The Guardian (Nigeria)
www.ngrguardiannews.com/
Independent Online (South Africa)
www.int.iol.co.za/
IPP Media (Tanzania)
http://www.ippmedia.com/
Le Messager (Cameroon) (Fr)
www.wagne.net/messager/
The Monitor (Uganda)
www.monitor.co.ug/
Walta (Ethiopia)
www.waltainfo.com/
El Watan (Algeria) (Fr)
www.elwatan.com/
Zimbabwe Independent
www.theindependent.co.zw/news/2006/January/Friday20/index.html

REFERENCES

Ainslie, R. (1966). *The press in Africa: Communications past and present*. London: Victor Gollancz.
Bamyeh, M. (2000). *The ends of globalization*. Minneapolis: University of Minnesota.
Barlow, J. (1999, January 12). "Tout ce que vous savez sur l'Afrique est faux" ("Everything you know about Africa is wrong"). *Jeune Afrique*, p. 30.
Bray, H. (2001a, July 22). "Africa goes online." *Boston Sunday Globe*, p. A1.

——— . (2001b, July 23). "Internet visionary hopes his plan has the e-touch." *Boston Globe*, p. A8.

Burnett, R., and Marshall, D. (2003). *Web theory*. London: Routledge.

Castells, M. (2000). *The rise of the network society*. 2nd ed. Malden, Mass.: Blackwell.

Clinton, W., and Gore, A. (1997). *A framework for electronic commerce*. Washington, D.C.: GPO.

Derrida, J. (1967). *Ecriture et la difference (Writing and difference)*. Paris: Universitaires de France.

Eko, L. (2001). "Many spiders, one World Wide Web: Toward a typology of Internet regulation." *Communication Law and Policy* 6, pp. 448–460.

——— (2003a). "Press freedom in Africa." In *Encyclopedia of international media and communication, vol. II*, pp. 95–116.

——— (2003b). "Between globalization and democratization: Governmental public broadcasting in Africa." In M. McCauley, E. Petersen, L. Artz, and D. D. Halleck (eds.), *Public broadcasting in the public interest*, pp. 175–191. Armonk, N.Y.: M. E. Sharpe.

——— (2003c). "Globalization and the mass media in Africa." In L. Artz and Y. Kamalipour (eds.), *The globalization of corporate media hegemony*, pp. 195–211. Albany: State University of New York.

——— (2004a). "Internet connectivity and development in Africa: Look before you leapfrog." In J. M. Mbaku and S. Saxena (eds.), *Africa at the crossroads*, pp. 211–231. Westport, Conn.: Praeger.

——— (2004b). "See all evil, hear all evil, rail against all evil: *Le Messager* and the journalism of resistance in Cameroon." In J. M. Mbaku and J. Takoungang (eds.), *The leadership challenge in Africa: Cameroon under Paul Biya*, pp. 123–151. Trenton, N.J.: Africa World.

——— (2004c). "Africa No. 1: Africa's first transnational commercial radio station." In *Encyclopedia of radio*, pp. 22–24. Chicago: Fitzroy Dearborn.

——— (2005, Spring/Summer). "Beasts of no nation: Re-presentation of African presidents in the post–Cold War African satirical press." *International Journal of Comic Art* 7(1), pp. 12–18.

El Pacho. (2002, May). "*Le Messager* popoli: Neuf ans déjà!" *Le Messager Popoli*, p. 7.

Enogo, O. (2001, October 2). "La BBC au Cameroun" ("The BBC comes to Cameroon"). *Jeune Afrique/L'Intelligent*, p. 2.

Foucault, M. (1994a). "Cours du 14 Janvier 1976" ("Lecture of January 14, 1976"). In D. Defert and M. Ewart (eds.), *Dits et ecrits par Michel Foucault (Sayings and writings of Michel Foucault)*, pp. 175–181. Paris: Gallimard.

——— (1994b). "Le sujet et le pouvoir" ("Subject and power"). In D. Defert and M. Ewart (eds.), *Dits et ecrits par Michel Foucault (Sayings and writings of Michel Foucault)*, pp. 222–242. Paris: Gallimard.

Geske, M. (2000). Globalization is what states make of it: Constructivism, U.S. foreign economic policy and the peso crisis. *International Policy* 37, pp. 301–322.

Geslin, J.-D. (2002, September 2). "L'info d'abord" ("Information first"). *Jeune Afrique*, pp. 72–77.

Giddens, A. (2000). *Runaway world: How globalization is shaping our lives*. New York: Routledge.

Gramsci, A. (1985). *Selections from the cultural writings.* D. Forgacs and G. Nowell-Smith (eds.); W. Boelhower (trans). Cambridge: Harvard University.
—— (1996). *Prison notebooks, vol. II* (first published in 1975). Joseph Buttigieg (ed. and trans). New York: Columbia University.
Held, D., and McGrew, A. (2002). *Globalization/anti-globalization.* Cambridge, UK: Polity.
Hountondji, P. (2000). "Cultures Africaines et mondialisation" ("African cultures and globalization"). In B. Duterme (ed.), *Cultures et mondialisation: Résistance and alternatives (Cultures and globalization: Resistance and alternatives)*, pp. 47–51. Paris: L'Harmattan.
Ibelema, M., Land, M., Eko, L., and Steyn, E. (2004). *Global journalism: Topical issues and media systems.* 4th ed. Boston: Allyn and Bacon.
Ihonvbere, J. (1997). "Democratization in Africa." *Peace Review* 9, pp. 371–378.
Ihonvbere, J., and Mbaku, J. M. (2003). "Establishing generalities and specificities in Africa's struggle for democracy and development." In J. O. Ihonvbere and J. M. Mbaku (eds.), *Political liberalization and democratization in Africa*, pp. 1–16. Westport, Conn.: Praeger.
Jensen, M. (2001). "Policies and strategies for accelerating Africa's information infrastructure development." In G. Nulens, N. Hafkins, L. Van Audenhove, and B. Cammaerts (eds.), *The digital divide in developing countries: Toward an information society in Africa*, pp. 130–160. Brussels: Brussels University.
Legrand, P. (2003). "The same and the different." In P. Legrand and R. Munday (eds.), *Comparative legal studies: Traditions and transitions*, pp. 240–311. Cambridge: Cambridge University.
Magubane, Z., and Zeleza, P. (2004). "Globalization and Africa's intellectual engagements." In M. Steger (ed.), *Rethinking globalism*, pp. 169–177. Lanham, Md.: Rowman and Littlefield.
Marson, I. (2004). "Open office gets the Zulu touch." *ZDNet UK.* At http://news.zdnet.co.uk (accessed May 30, 2005).
Mason, A. (2001). "Cartoon journalism in Africa puts political power into perspective." *Media Development* 68, pp. 50–53.
Mattelart, A. (2002). *La mondialisation de la communication (Globalization of communication).* Paris: Universitaires de France.
Mbaku, J. M. (1997). *Institutions and reform in Africa: The public choice perspective.* Westport, Conn.: Praeger.
Mbembe, A. (2001). *On the postcolony.* Berkeley: University of California.
Meunier, S. (2000, August 3). "The hegemonic hamburger." *Wilson Quarterly* 24, pp. 120–121.
Mittelman, J. (2004). *Whither globalization? The vortex of knowledge and ideology.* New York: Routledge.
Monga, C. (1996). *The anthropology of anger: Civil society and democracy in Africa.* Boulder: Lynne Rienner.
Monge, P., and Contractor, N. (2003). *Theories of communication networks.* Oxford: Oxford University.
Moulson, G. (2000, August 3). "Big tobacco documents show who targeted." *Bangor Daily News*, p. A5.

Ndao, A. (2003). *Comprendre et traiter la societé de l'information. (Understanding the information society)*. Dakar, Senegal: Panos Institute West Africa.

Nelken, D. (2003). "Comparatists and transferability." In P. Le Grand and R. Munday (eds.), *Comparative Legal Studies: Traditions and Transitions*, pp. 437–466. Cambridge: Cambridge University.

Ngenda, A. (2005). "The nature of the international intellectual property system: Universal norms and values or Western chauvinism?" *Information and Communication Technology Law* 14(1), pp. 59–80.

Ogundimu, F. F. (1996). "Private-enterprise broadcasting and accelerating dependency: Case studies from Nigerian and Uganda." *Gazette* 58, pp. 159–172.

Opoku-Mensah, A. (2001). "Democratizing access through the information society." In G. Nulens, N. Hafkins, L. Van Audenhove, and B. Cammaerts (eds.), *The digital divide in developing countries: Toward an information society in Africa*, pp. 161–196. Brussels: Brussels University.

Reno v. ACLU, 521 U.S. 844 (1997).

Reporters Without Borders. (2002). *Gabon-Annual Report 2002*. At www.rsf.org/article.php?id_article=1837 (accessed January 15, 2005).

SAT-3/WASC/SAFE Submarine Cable System (2004). At www.safe-sat3.co.za/HomePage/SAT3_WASC_SAFE_Home.asp.

Shah, R., and Kesan, J. (2003). "Manipulating the governance characteristics of code." *Info* 5(4), pp. 3–9.

Slouka, M. (1995). *War of the worlds*. New York: BasicBooks.

U.S. AID (1999). *U.S. AID Leland initiative: African global information infrastructure project*. At www.info.USAID.Gov/leland (accessed January 2005).

U.S. Congress. House. HR 415, 105th Cong., 2nd sess., *Congressional Record* 144 (1998): H 7655.

Van Audenhove, L., Burgelman, J., Nulens, G., and Cammaerts, B., eds. (2001). "Telecommunication and information society policy in Africa." In *The digital divide in developing countries: Toward an information society in Africa*, pp. 17–54. Brussels: Brussels University.

VOA (Voice of America). (2005). At www.voanews.com/affiliates/about_affiliates.cfm.

Waltremez, E. (1992). "The satirical press in francophone Africa." *Index on Censorship* 21, pp. 34–36.

Wendt, A. (1992). "Anarchy is what states make of it: The social structure of power politics." *International Organization* 46, pp. 391–425.

Zulu, B. (1996). "Rebuilding Africa through film, video, and television." In P. G. Altbach and S. Hassan (eds.), *The muse of modernity: Essays on culture as development in Africa*, pp. 63–78. Trenton, N.J.: Africa World.

2

◆

Asia: The Hollywood Factor

Kuldip R. Rampal

Market expansion has spread rapidly over the last decade with the international deregulation of trade, spurred by the dissolution of the Soviet Union and the planned economies of the Eastern Bloc in the 1990s, and the economic initiatives of leading capitalist nations through the World Economic Forum, the International Monetary Fund, and the World Bank. In the wake of deregulation, privatization, and commercialization of industry, trade, and culture internationally, commercial media models and markets have created more consumers of media entertainment than ever before. The rising literacy levels in Asian countries and increased access to Western (mostly American) entertainment offerings are leading media audiences to look beyond their traditional cultural practices and national entertainment industries. Throughout Asia, even the casual visitor must observe the pervasiveness of American culture, imported through a variety of media, especially movies and television programming, and increasingly the Internet. The *Washington Post* reported that international sales of American entertainment and software products totaled $60.2 billion in 1996, more than any other U.S. industry ("American pop" 1998).

Important questions emerge from this phenomenon: What are the implications of Western media globalization for indigenous cultures in developing Asian countries? What kind of influence, if any, is Western media globalization having on indigenous media industries? In this age of media globalization, are there any indications that cultural influences may be taking place both ways—between the East and the West—rather than only from the West to the East? This chapter addresses these questions by focusing on the film industries of several Asian countries and Hollywood.

CULTURAL DEPENDENCY, MEDIA GROWTH:
THEORETICAL CONSIDERATIONS

Expansion of democracy and economic liberalization since the 1990s has also unleashed unparalleled Western cultural influences around the world. This has raised concerns among social critics and policymakers in many countries. Omar Biggins says, "Globalization, with an adverse advocacy through the media, has brought in a landslide transformation of existing local culture and identity into a new form of culture with no frontier" (2004 p. 4). Jerry Mander, cofounder of the International Forum on Globalization, has voiced the same concern. Writing in *The Nation*, Mander said that global media corporations, owned by Rupert Murdoch, Ted Turner, and very few others, "transmit their Western images and commercial values directly into the brains of 75 percent of the world's population. The globalization of media imagery is surely the most effective means ever for cloning cultures to make them compatible with the Western corporate vision" (1996).

Biggins cites the cultural dependency theory of Mohammadi (1995) as a factor in the influence of the Western culture in the developing world. He quotes Mohammadi as follows:

> The continuance of Western dominance over Third World nations was based partly on advanced technologies, including communication technologies. But it was also based on an ideology, accepted in many parts of the Third World, that there was only one path to economic development, which was to imitate the process of development of Western industrial capitalist societies. Cultural imperialism or cultural dependency occurs with the Western countries' influence on the language, values and attitudes (including religion), ways of organizing public life, styles of politics, forms of education, and professional training, clothing styles, and many other cultural habits. It creates a new kind of model of domination called neocolonialism which has sparked new kinds of struggles to eradicate this enduring cultural influence in the Third World. (Biggins 2004, p. 4)

American author Herbert Schiller had cautioned back in 1969 that the implications of the cultural influences brought about by American programming were far-reaching, especially for developing peoples of the world. "Everywhere local culture is facing submersion from the mass-produced outpourings of commercial broadcasting in the United States," he said, adding, "To foster consumerism in the poor world [through American entertainment programming] sets the stage for frustration on a massive scale" (Schiller 1969, p. 111).

Apart from the cultural dependency theory, at least two other factors must also be considered in explaining the influence of Western, especially American, media on indigenous media industries in developing countries. First, the lowest-common-denominator production principle of American entertainment industries, which gears content for mass audiences, has been found to be the most successful for maximizing sales, circulation, and advertising revenues (Lowenstein and Merrill 1990, p. 33). This principle is aimed at pandering to the basic, pleasure-seeking instincts in human beings through the themes of sex, violence, and alcohol in media content, a formula long used by Hollywood and a mainstay of the established-studio productions. The rise of the independent film industry in the United States is attributed to a rejection of the Hollywood production formula. In recent years, a more degenerated form of the lowest-common-denominator production formula has been seen in the tabloidization of television shows such as the *Jerry Springer Show*.

Second, economic globalization and increasing industrialization in developing Asian countries have facilitated a rise in income levels for people in these countries, resulting in an expanding consumer base for both print and electronic media. The history of media development in the West shows that media transform from offering a high-level content to a relatively small consumer base in preindustrial societies to a relatively low-level, popular-appeal type of content to serve the needs and interests of an expanding, but not well-educated, consumer base in industrializing societies, as evidenced by the rise of the sensational penny press in early 1800s in the United States. This evolutionary model of media growth in all societies is offered as the elite-popular-specialized theory of media progression (Lowenstein and Merrill 1990, pp. 31–33). These theoretical considerations and the cultural dependency theory will serve as the backdrop in explaining the reshaping of film industries in several Asian countries.

THE HOLLYWOODIZATION OF MOVIE INDUSTRIES IN ASIA

India

India's film industry, based primarily in the western city of Bombay and nicknamed "Bollywood," provides perhaps the most compelling example of an Asian film industry's incorporation of the Hollywood production formula in recent years. India's movie industry, which turns out more than 800 feature films a year in a variety of languages (Pendakur 2003,

p. 2) as compared to about 250 produced by Hollywood annually (Plate 2002), is the largest in the world. However, while Hollywood earned almost $10 billion, Bollywood generated only about $2 billion in 2002 ("Where are the storytellers" 2003). In recent years, movie theater attendance in India has fallen substantially, because the industry's traditional song-and-dance storylines, rehash of old and tired scripts, and hackneyed treatment of love scenes have not produced big hits. As a result, the film industry has increasingly started to copy Hollywood's sex, alcohol, and action-oriented formula rather than its creativity. Since the early part of this decade, Bollywood has been openly dealing with sex and offering generous doses of skin in an attempt to draw audiences. As the British news agency Reuters reported on October 21, 2004, "Daring young actors and actresses have thrown caution, and their clothes, to the wind to play amorous characters such as prostitutes, adulterers, playboys and husband swappers that Bollywood rarely touched in the past" ("Bollywood finds" Oct. 21, 2004). This new approach to filmmaking appears to be having positive economic results.

For example, Agence-France Presse reported that the biggest grossing film in 2003 was Bollywood's *Jism* (*Body*), which tells the story of a woman who is unapologetic about using her sexuality to persuade her lover to kill her rich husband. The small budget film turned out to be a surprise hit and its star, Bipasha Basu, became one of the most sought after actresses in Bollywood. "The success of *Jism* showed that Indians are no longer ashamed of watching a steamy scene in a full house," said leading filmmaker Mahesh Bhatt, who wrote the film's screenplay. Bhatt said the film reflected a change in the mind-set of the Indian viewer. "Earlier, a steamy film would be shown in small towns and would be seen by men who came for titillation, but now urban women throng upscale halls to watch such films" ("Bollywood turns" 2003).

Julie, a Hindi film released in summer 2004, deals with the subject of prostitution, played by a top beauty queen, Neha Dhupia. Her character ends up as a prostitute after her boyfriends leave her after sleeping with her. The movie was a box office hit for repeatedly showing lovemaking scenes, turning the actress into a new sensation among moviegoers. *Girlfriend*, also released in 2004, deals with lesbianism and contained a brief erotic scene between two women. There were violent protests in sections of the country, as the generally conservative Indian society, and critics, decried the film. But the movie was still playing and another lesbian-themed film was said to be in the works.

Other recent films like *Oops* and *Boom* have also caused a lot of controversy in India. *Oops* explores the murky world of male strippers, which, says movie critic Prathamesh Menon, is a concept so vague and unfamiliar to the Indian audience that there was rioting in some cinema theaters in an attempt to ban the film (Menon 2003). *Boom* shows its three female leads strutting through most of the two-hour film in little more than bikinis; in the film, the leads are frequently the target of crude sexual remarks. One male lead asks a woman to perform oral sex under his desk as he works. Menon says that elsewhere in the world that might be considered relatively tame stuff, but not in India where even smooching in public can still cause outrage.

For many years, Bollywood films shied away from showing even a kiss, with scenes chastely cutting away to shots of birds, bees, or flowers. However, the 2003 release *Khwaish* (*Desire*) showed not less than seventeen kissing scenes and portrayed a young couple who are anything but shy about discussing their sex life. *Murder* and *Andaaz*, other recently released films, have generated a lot of buzz, not over their actresses' acting abilities, but rather over their skimpy clothing and kissing scenes.

Taran Adarsh, a Bollywood critic, explained this new phenomenon in moviemaking. "Sex sells. And it works well if it comes with a good story. Cable TV has brought in a lot of Western influences to Indian homes. People are more accepting and more open now," he said ("Bollywood finds" Oct. 21, 2004). Bollywood producer and upcoming director Rashika Singh offered another explanation. She said filmmakers in India are increasingly targeting the urban youth audience. "The younger viewers want their idols to dance like Michael Jackson, swagger like Tom Cruise, fight like Jackie Chan—and still croon to their beloved in Swiss meadows, and deliver rhetorical dialogue with panache! It is like having your Indian cake and licking the forbidden Western icing too" (Menon 2003). One of India's leading sociologists, Shiv Vishwanathan, said the new face of Bollywood is a bit of art imitating life. "It's thanks to globalization," he said, referring to the Western-market economic path India switched to in 1991, "opening up to multinational firms, satellite TV and easier international travel" ("Bollywood finds" Oct. 21, 2004).

Social critics, however, worry about the likely implications of the new trend in Bollywood filmmaking for Indian society. Traditionally, Bollywood enthralled Indians globally with song-and-dance extravaganzas and melodramatic stories big on family values. Generally, the Indian film industry has not had a background in realism and the plot has been kept simple so that even the rural villager could easily relate to it. The new Hollywood-inspired shift in film style is seen to be a threat to the values and culture of the Indian people. The current Bollywood formula has some cause for concern because the transplantation of Western ideas has led to extreme vulgarity with high sexual innuendo and unnecessary violence. As Indian film actress Deepti Naval says, "Vulgarity in Hindi songs today shows that filmmakers take the audience to be buffoons and even a little retarded. I call today's age as the 'pelvic age,' where hero and heroine simply gyrate to the music" ("Deepti" 1999, p. 8). The Film Federation of India, which regulates film content, also complains that new Bollywood films are too Westernized and are degrading and diminishing India's true cultural identity.

Another cause for concern, from the standpoint of creativity and ethics, is Bollywood's tendency in recent years to copy themes from popular Hollywood films. The 2004 Bollywood hit movie *Aitraaz* so blatantly copies the 1994 Hollywood movie *Disclosure* that, despite its poor attempt to give the plot a local twist, the credibility and ethics of the new Bollywood are thrown into question. *Aitraaz* is a courtroom drama featuring a young telecommunications executive who is taken to court by his female boss and former lover after the boss's attempts to revive her affair with the young executive are rebuffed. "If you point to any new Bollywood release," says movie critic Menon, "you can bet that there existed a Hollywood original somewhere down the line. This highlights the worrying dependency of the industry on its Hollywood counterpart" (Menon 2003). Disillusioned by this trend, noted film producer-director Mahesh Bhatt said that "Bollywood has run out of new ideas and is going through the throes of 'creative death'" (Bhatt Nov. 4, 2004). Bhatt mentioned the continuing popularity of stories and storytellers in India. "It is time our filmmakers went back to the roots, resurrected good storytellers and paid attention to originality," he said.

There are indications that at least some in the industry are beginning to take that advice seriously. As Bollywood producers and directors realize that action-sex-drugs themes devoid of genuinely creative scripts are losing audience appeal, the industry is beginning to evolve to the next stage of filmmaking to turn around its economic decline. Chopra says that a new type of Hindi cinema is emerging, one which is composed of smaller, offbeat films that are more realistic than Bollywood tales and edgier than art-house ones. "These films have none of the overt glamour or sunny disposition of mainstream movies. Emotions are messy, characters have pasts and endings aren't always happy" (Chopra 2005).

For example, *Page 3*, the first hit movie of 2005, provides a scathing look at high society in Bombay. It features pedophilia, drug-fueled rave parties, and unabashed nastiness. Chopra says the film, made for $575,000, grossed $2.3 million in India—a stellar performance, even though it did not have what Bollywood insiders call "face value" (like stars or hit songs). *Being Cyrus*, another 2005 release, has been described as a "dark, unsettling film" about the members of a dysfunctional Parsi family who let a stranger into their lives, with dire consequences. Interestingly, another American phenomenon—multiplexes—is fueling the rise of this independent film industry because multiplex viewers are culturally and economically more upscale than the general audience. There are 73 multiplexes in India, with 276 screens, and about 89,470 seats. These numbers are expected to increase to 135 multiplexes with more than 160,000 seats by the end of 2006 (Chopra 2005).

Japan

The other large Asian film industry, indeed the second largest in the world after India, is the Japanese film industry, which is also trying to reinvent itself in the wake of cultural globalization. Movie critic Donald Richie, in his book *A Hundred Years of Japanese Film*, cites the historic influence of Hollywood on one of Japan's leading studios, Shochiku Company, founded in 1895. Richie says that the Shochiku directors were profoundly influenced by American movies, with their creative editing techniques and linear, suspense-driven plots. Shochiku's leading director Yasujiro Ozu cited Ernst Lubitsch's 1924 movie, *The Marriage Circle*, as one of his strongest influences. Richie adds that one can see much of Lubitsch's crispness, speed, and concision in Ozu's *Fighting Friends, Japanese Style* and *A Straightforward Boy* ("Tokyo on the Hudson" 2005).

Japan has been historically prominent in the global entertainment business, especially in the three decades following World War II, when film masters such as Akira Kurosawa, Yasujiro Ozu, and Kenji Mizoguchi were treasured throughout the world. Remakes of notable Japanese titles, such as *Seven Samurai*, served as a source for Hollywood studio releases. However, the samurai series of films, which were swordplay classics of the 1950s, 1960s, and 1970s, began to lose their luster in the 1980s. Kagon says the Japanese film industry began a downturn in the 1990s because of a new, global popular culture and digital revolution. She says that filmmakers are now challenged to tell stories that interest a cosmopolitan domestic and international audience even as they try to retain and convey unique, indigenous, cultural characteristics. In addition, anyone with a digital camera, a computer, access to the Internet, enough energy, and an idea (a quality idea is not a prerequisite) can become a filmmaker, says Kagon. "The winners in this 'new game' will be independent filmmakers and media companies which create transnationally appealing content," she says (Kagon 2005).

Japanese producers released 310 movies in 2004, but the country still imported 339 films that year, including 152 from the United States. Foreign films accounted for 60 percent of box office revenues, and of the top 20 earners in 2004, 13 were foreign films and only 7 were domestic. Of the top 7 domestic earners, 4 were animations and 2 were romances (JETRO 2005). According to Kenji Ishizaka, film coordinator of the Japan Foundation and film teacher at Waseda University, soft-core pornography called *pink films* made up almost half of the Japanese output in 2003 ("The sun rises" 2004).

The Japanese film industry, however, entered a steady recovery phase in 2004. Ishizaka says many critics are confounded by the huge success of the Takeshi Kitano movies, "whose violence and twistedness evoke comparisons with movies of [American director] Quentin Tarantino." Kitano's movies seem to combine film noir and the samurai genre though in ruggedly contemporary form. "All of this shows that the more successful Japanese movies build on the successes of the past, but also inject a contemporary spirit on the old" (*Philippine Daily Inquirer* Nov. 29, 2004). Also, as in India, the rise of the multiplex phenomenon is helping the resurgence of movie viewing. Multiplexes accounted for more than 60 percent of all screens in Japan as of May 2005, which has led to more Japanese films being shown without going through a major distributor (JETRO 2005).

Remarkably, the turnaround of the Japanese film industry, which has been attributed to a good measure of Hollywood influence, is helping Hollywood in return. Remakes of highly successful Japanese films are being released by Hollywood once again. For example, Japanese horror films are taking the world by storm. Hideo Nakata directed the original 1998 movie *Ringu*, one of the most popular films in Japanese cinema history, and *Ringu 2*, which was even more successful. The Hollywood remake of *Ringu* as *The Ring*, produced by Steven Spielberg's DreamWorks studio, directed by Gore Verbinki and starring Naomi Watts, was even bigger in 2002 (Phelan April 3, 2005). Takashi Shimizu's 2003 release *Ju-on* was remade as *The Grudge* by Hollywood in 2004. Other highly successful Japanese-inspired Hollywood releases in recent years include the *Kill Bill* series, *The Last Samurai*, and *The Blind Swordsman*. As Larsen notes, "Hollywood is embracing Asian cinema because the films are stylish and have smart stories" (Larsen 2005).

South Korea

The resurgence of the South Korean film industry in the late 1990s is also attributed to integrating the Hollywood sex, action-thriller approach to the indigenous cinematic style. Today's South Korean films showcase high production values boasting atmospheric cinematography and Tinseltown-style special effects. Output has risen since 1998, with seventy-four movies released in 2004. Replacing indifferent business conglomerates, small independents and five major sales-and-distribution companies now rule the industry (Chan 2004; Australian Film Commission 2005). Throughout South Korea's film history, the melodrama has dominated popular film. In any given year, from 50 to 70 percent of the films produced in South Korea are classified, rather broadly, as melodramas. Popular movie stars are often best remembered for their roles in heart-wrenching tragedies. In recent years, however, South Korean cinema has reinvented itself, reclaiming its own domestic market from Hollywood productions. Paquet (2000) says there are several ways in which the films of today have tried to distance themselves from their predecessors. Newer films tend to have a glossier feel to them, and as the technical capabilities of the industry have expanded, directors have started to employ sophisticated digital imagery and special effects. Gary Mak, associate director of Hong Kong's Broadway Cinematheque, says contemporary South Korean films are more explicitly violent, and directors have a habit of including sex scenes whether they fit the plot or not. "In terms of sex, Koreans can be much bolder than Chinese," he says, giving as an example Lee Ji-sang's 1998 movie *Yellow Flower,* featured in film festivals abroad but banned in South Korea until 2002 because of its graphic sex scenes (Walker 2004).

Paquet says the 1999 thriller *Shiri,* for example, shrewdly combines the Hollywood action blockbuster with the Korean melodrama to result in a film that appeals to a wide spectrum of viewers. A dazzling action movie, *Shiri* follows two South Korean government agents, Ryu and Lee, as they pursue a female super-assassin from North Korea. Very stylish and realistic, *Shiri* represents a smooth fusion of Hong Kong and American action movies. This was the first film in South Korean history to sell more than two million tickets in Seoul alone. It smashed the domestic box-office record previously held by *Titanic* to become the most successful Korean film ever.

Citing another example, Paquet says that director Lee Myung-se's previous works have centered on issues of love and marriage (e.g., *My Love, My Bride,* released in 1990, and *First Love,* released in 1993). However, in his 1999 *Nowhere to Hide,* the director takes a seeming change of course by choosing the action genre. Action films, a hallmark of Hollywood, typically feature a continuous level of high energy, stunts, chase scenes, fights, escapes, rescues, nonstop motion, an unbroken storyline, and a resourceful hero struggling against incredible odds to defeat an evil villain. Paquet notes that many aspects of *Nowhere to Hide* fit this description: the film centers on a group of detectives who struggle to catch a wanted assassin and features chase scenes (one in which the detective is barefoot), fights (often notable for their striking visuals and humor), disguises, killings, and narrow escapes (2000).

This success of South Korean films has attracted the attention of Hollywood. Films such as *Shiri* are now distributed in the USA, and in 2001 Miramax bought the rights to an Americanized remake of the successful Korean film *My Wife Is a Gangster.* The 2003 suspense thriller *Janghwa, Hongnyeon (Tale of Two Sisters)* was successful as well, leading DreamWorks to pay $2 million for the rights to a remake, topping the $1 million paid for the rights to remake the Japanese movie *Ringu* ("Korean films" 2004). DreamWorks also snapped up the remake rights for the 2001 film *My Sassy Girl*, which was South Korea's highest-grossing comedy. Its script about a domineering, volatile woman and her hapless boyfriend was such a hit in Hong Kong that it pulled in $14 million—making it one of the most successful South Korean films (Walker 2004).

China and Hong Kong

For ideological reasons, the Chinese film industry had been highly regulated by the state and served as a propaganda organ. It largely remains so in spite of the government's efforts to calibrate the industry with the ongoing policy of economic liberalization. Following its accession to the World Trade Organization in late 2001, China is also obligated to open up its entertainment business to imports from overseas. To compete with overseas productions, China has launched a restructuring process for its own movie industry. Jihong and Kraus say the reforms have borrowed explicitly from the principles by which Hollywood is organized. With direct government involvement, the Chinese film industry actively imitates the Hollywood system; the entire industry is undergoing full-scale commercialization along with a vertical integration of production, distribution, and exhibition sectors, and a linkage of film and television interests. The reform of the film industry is not welcomed by all. Many Communist Party propagandists are reluctant to give up control over such an important medium (Jihong and Kraus 2002). The Chinese film industry produced one hundred films in 2004.

The number of domestic productions in the Chinese territory of Hong Kong has steadily declined since 2001, when Hong Kong released 144 films. Only 64 films were produced in 2004 (Australian Film Commission 2005). This one-time major film industry of the world is seeing Hollywood's influence also. For example, borrowing from the *Mission: Impossible* movies, the Hong Kong production *Downtown Torpedoes*, released in 1997, is the story of a team called ATM (Advanced Tactical Mercenaries) that performs high-risk industrial theft "jobs." Directed by Teddy Chan, this film offers fast-paced action, excellent editing, and daring stunts rather than the mushy love story typical of many Hong Kong productions. Like the *Mission Impossible* movies, there are a fair number of double-crosses, hidden agents, and other plot twists in this film. A review by a Hong Kong critic noted that *Downtown Torpedoes* is "a stylish movie that shows that HK film-makers can take some inspiration from the US without totally diluting their product. It's not a classic, but compared to crud like *Tokyo Raiders* or this movie's pseudo-sequel *Skyline Cruisers*, it's a refreshing change" ("Downtown torpedoes" 2004).

Indeed, Hollywood's influence on Asian film industries seems most effective when it takes place within a framework of local traditions and culture. An interesting example is that of Hong Kong action-film director John Woo. Feaster notes that Woo adopts American director Sam Peckinpah's machismo, but also combines it with his traditional Chinese sensibilities, which show a deep appreciation for honor and loyalty and the willingness to die for a friend (2002). That cinematic style was hailed in Woo films, including *Hard Boiled, The Killer,* and *Bullet in the Head,* exported to the West. Woo followed the same style in the Hollywood production of his war film *Windtalkers,* starring Nicholas Cage and Christian Slater. Feaster says that through this cinematic style, "Woo brought something fresh and exciting to American audiences while also recharging a genre that often slid into cancerous nihilism in the hands of brutal action heroes like Charles Bronson, Clint Eastwood and Arnold Schwarzenegger" (2002).

Also in the best Hollywood tradition, Hong Kong director Ang Lee combined an all-star lineup and top technical talent in his *Crouching Tiger, Hidden Dragon.* An epic set against the breathtaking landscapes of ancient China, this highly successful film combines the exhilarating martial arts choreography of Yuen Wo-Pind (*The Matrix*) with the sensitivity and classical storytelling of an Ang Lee film. When the film was released to American movie theaters in December 2000, it marked the peak of what many American film reviewers and film critics have been calling an "Asian invasion" in Hollywood.

The Philippines

Another significant movie industry in Southeast Asia is that of the Philippines, which produced sixty films in 2004, although the country produced ninety-seven films in 2002. This was larger than the film industries of neighboring Indonesia and Malaysia, which produced twenty-one and twenty-two films in 2004, respectively (Australian Film Commission 2005). An interesting explanation of the influence of Hollywood on the Filipino movie industry was offered at the 2003 Sangandan Film Festival in the Philippines. In a forum on Hollywood's influence on Filipino films, a film expert said, "since local viewers get to see mostly American productions, they are bearers of the USA's cultural imprint, and have been 'subliminally' programmed to prefer big blockbusters to the more intimate and personal dramas that European filmmakers prefer to produce" ("Hollywoodization of Thai" 2004). It was further noted at the forum that after the American occupation of the Philippines in the early part of the twentieth century, most of the imported films came from the United States.

"This was colonizers' way of holding up U.S.–related ideals before our grandfathers' eyes, so that, in due time, Filipino filmmakers aped American film products in their own productions," said a film expert ("Hollywoodization of Thai" 2004). "Thus, the preference for fair-skinned, aquiline-nosed stars, clear-cut conflicts between true-blue heroes and dastardly villains, forthright storytelling, 'moral lessons,' 'message' films, and filmmaking conventions that still characterize some of our movies today," the film expert added. This preference was said to make it difficult for small local movies to be released or distributed in the country. This also ups the ante when it comes to movie budgets and is another factor preventing independent companies or self-financed filmmakers from making much headway in the local movie scene.

Thailand

In his study of Thai cinema, Sukothai Open University resident film expert Kamjohn Louiyapong chronicles the advances in technology and the influence of foreign films, especially Japanese productions such as *Ringu* and *Ju-on* and their Hollywood remakes, *The Ring* and *The Grudge* ("Bring out the dead" 2005). As a result of the new technology and the influence of foreign films, the fledgling Thai film industry is beginning to take off. The country produced only fifteen films in 2001; however, that number jumped to forty-seven in 2004 (Australian Film Commission 2005). Ghost stories, for example, have been committed to celluloid no less than a score of times before, but with the 1999 release *Nang Nak* (*Ghost Wife*), director Nonzee Nimibutr dragged Thai ghost movies kicking and screaming into the modern world. The film has been described by critics as blending stunning attention to period detail, lush locations, slick pacing, and clever use of flashbacks with the bravura performances the director coaxed from his stars ("Bring out the dead" 2005). It is a tale of a woman who dies in childbirth after her husband leaves to go to war against the Burmese. So strong is her love that she stays around in spirit form. Her husband returns home and resumes wedded bliss with his wife, not realizing she is no longer of this world. *Nang Nak* set box office records in Thailand and even managed to outsell James Cameron's *Titanic* in that country.

Louiyapong, of the Sukothai Open University, said *Nang Nak* represents a shift to a more modern way of moviemaking. "In the past five or six years, these influences have allowed directors to narrate ghost stories in a more chilling and fun way, and have also opened the films up to some broader social and cultural discourses from academics," he said.

In *Beautiful Boxer*, a highly successful 2003 release, director Ekachai Uekrongtham adopts the action-drama approach. Based on the true story of Thailand's famed transgender kickboxer, Nong Thoom, *Beautiful Boxer* is an incredible tale of an effeminate boy who fights like a man so he can become a woman. Believing since childhood that he is a girl trapped in a boy's body, Nong Thoom, played by Parinya Charoenphol, sets out to master the most masculine and lethal sport of Muaythai (Thai boxing) to earn a living and to achieve his ultimate goal of total femininity.

Critics have described the film as touching, funny, and packed with breathtaking Thai kickboxing sequences. Following its screening at the 2004 Bangkok Film Festival, which drew the likes of Oliver Stone and Colin Farrell from Hollywood, the film was widely expected to get international distribution. A number of other recent Thai films were also said to have been sold to U.S. distributors ("Hollywoodization of Thai" 2004).

ASIAN VALUES VS. HOLLYWOOD VALUES: A DIALECTIC

Most academic debates since the new world information order movement of the 1970s on the implications of the dominance of Western media for non-Western countries have warned of imminent dangers to indigenous cultures. The foregoing analysis of the reshaping of some of the Asian film industries seems to lend some support to that view. But the analysis also indicates that Asian cinema can benefit when it takes into account the larger dynamics of Hollywood's success—its creativity, technique, and editing style rather than focusing only on the Hollywood "formula" of sex, violence, action, and drugs.

Bollywood is a typical case study. Although the success of the sex and nudity–oriented Bollywood films confirms that there is a Westernized audience in India with an appetite for such films, India is still largely a rural country, and farmers and villagers provide a vital contribution to the economy of the film industry. They cannot possibly understand and appreciate the values and issues expressed by the new Bollywood. Social critics in India are also worried that by entering the mainstream adult movie market, the uniqueness of Bollywood in providing elaborate family-oriented musical dramas will be lost. They also caution that apart from threatening traditional Indian values, the industry will become more vulnerable to outside competition, which in turn may damage Bollywood beyond repair.

The dilemma faced by Bollywood in maintaining the economic viability of the industry on the one hand and protecting and serving traditional Indian values on the other is resulting in serious soul-searching regarding the direction the industry should take. One view comes from a highly successful new Bollywood director, Ram Gopal Varma. The Asian edition of *Time* magazine in its cover story on Bollywood in October 2003 quoted Varma as saying, "anyone who does not follow the West is gone" (Perry

2003). Varma also noted that he did not care whether his movies served the needs of the rural, traditional Indian population. Indian superstar Aamir Khan responded to that view by warning that a wholesale rejection of song and dance might kill the "color, fire and innocence" that defines Indian cinema (Perry 2003).

Another view comes from writer Pankaj Mishra, who suggests incorporating the Hollywood style to filmmaking without straying too far from Bollywood's usual version of the romantic triangle. This would echo the action-drama style adopted by Hong Kong director John Woo and the Korean and Thai filmmakers, as discussed earlier. Mishra cites the *Kal Ho Na Ho* (*Tomorrow May Never Come*), released in 2003, as an example. The movie, set entirely in New York, brings a new slickness to Bollywood dreams of affluence and style—while singing, the characters combine Hindi lyrics with the rhythms of disco, rap, and gospel—but it simultaneously reaffirms family through a gregarious cast of brothers, sisters, parents, grandmothers, and grandfathers. To Mishra, such films are "becoming the echo chamber of middle-class India as it tries to bend—without breaking—its old, austere culture of underdevelopment" (Mishra 2004).

EMERGING ASIAN MOVIE MARKETS AND IMPLICATIONS FOR HOLLYWOOD

Research indicates there are at least two important implications of the new phenomena gripping Asian film producers. First, Hollywood may itself benefit from the increasing Hollywoodization, albeit within local sociocultural frameworks, of indigenous film industries in Asia. As mentioned above, Hollywood is increasingly remaking highly successful Asian films, as the case studies of Japan, Korea, and Hong Kong demonstrate. In addition, as MIT professor Christina Klein notes, "Hollywood today is going into the business of producing and distributing 'foreign' movies. This move derives from studio executives' suspicion that Hollywood films may have reached the limits of their overseas appeal. As evidence, they point to the growing popularity of locally made films around the world" (Klein 2003).

Klein says Hollywood is finding ways to turn a profit on the desires of audiences to see local films; rather than trying to beat the competition, the studios are joining it. In the last few years, Columbia, Warner Brothers, Disney/Buena Vista, Miramax, and Universal have all created special overseas divisions or partnerships to produce and distribute films in languages other than English. The Sony-owned Columbia Pictures subsidiary in Hong Kong, for example, has produced a number of films in Chinese.

Hollywood studios are also becoming important financiers and distributors of Asian films. This trend has contributed to the success of Asian filmmakers, such as Indian director Mira Nair, whose 2001 hit, *Monsoon Wedding*, was distributed by Universal Studios in the United States. Nair's latest production, *The Namesake*, adapted from the novel of the London-born, New York–based Indian writer Jhumpa Lahiri, is directed by an Indian, has American, Indian, and Japanese financing, and is shot extensively in Calcutta and New York ("On the world's movie map" 2005, p. 75).

In addition, the increasing globalization of film industries is making it possible for "foreign" movie stars to make their mark in America. Indian beauty queen and film star Aishwarya Rai, for example, has appeared in her first movie in English, *Bride and Prejudice*, which was distributed by Miramax in the United States in late 2004. Klein says the Hong Kong film industry alone has contributed actors like Jackie Chan, Jet Li, and Chow Yun-fat; directors such as Tsui Hark, Kirk Wong, and Ringo Lam; and martial arts choreographers like Yuen Wo Ping, Yuen Cheung-yan, and Corey Yuen.

In short, transnationalization of the movie industry throughout Asia is altering strictly national-cultural activities in ways that has yet to be fully revealed, although certainly the production and distribution companies prefer market-driven, export-capable films. While domestic, culturally and language-specific movies better attract national audiences, the content, narrative, and stylistic flourishes of films throughout the region now seem to have a tendency to mimic the Hollywood model of individualism, action, and quick-and-easy narrative resolution.

The second implication of the Hollywoodization of Asian filmmaking regards the future of Hollywood itself. In view of the increasing globalization of filmmaking, and with China and India projected to be larger movie markets than Europe, will Hollywood remain immune to Asian influences on its own style of filmmaking? The answer seems to be no in view of the economic factor. Klein says from the 1950s through the 1970s, Hollywood earned about 30 percent of its money overseas. "That number is expected to grow over time, with some industry figures predicting the foreign share of box office earnings could rise to 80 percent within the next twenty years. This means that Hollywood is becoming an export industry, making movies primarily for people who live outside the US" (Klein 2003). Asia alone is expected to be responsible for as much as 60 percent of Hollywood's box-office revenue by then.

This market reality is expected to result in an increasing crossover of Asian cinematic style into Hollywood. As Klein says, when scholars talk about global cinema, they usually mean the Hollywood blockbusters that perform well in markets around the world—films like *Titanic* or *Jurassic Park* (2003). But the integration of Hollywood and Asian film industries is producing a different kind of global cinema: films that contain material and stylistic elements from industries on both sides of the Pacific. *Hero,* China's official submission for the 2002 foreign-language Academy Award, is one example of this new global cinema. Menon says an example of the successful globalization of both Eastern and Western film styles can be seen when Hollywood takes on the ideas of Bollywood (2003). "When Australian director Baz Lurman was filming *Moulin Rouge,* he commented that his intention was to apply the 'Bollywood masala' formula. When [Indian] director Shekhar Kapur shot *Elizabeth,* he insisted that it have all the kinetic color of a Bollywood film. Kapur was also the producer for the recent Bollywood-style romantic comedy, *The Guru,* complete with dance numbers and dream scenes. New releases like *Bollywood Queen* and *Bride and Prejudice* also intend to apply this formula," says Menon.

Production-cost reduction is another benefit Hollywood can expect in the globalizing film industry. As the newsweekly magazine *India Today* notes in its August 15, 2005, issue, outsourcing postproduction work from Hollywood and European film industries to India is picking up because it makes commercial sense. "India has great infrastructure, skilled and cost-effective labour and diverse locations," the magazine quotes Emmanuel Pappas of On The Road Productions as saying (p. 76). "In the past two years, there has been a 100 percent jump in work being outsourced to India," the article notes (p. 76). Indeed, because of low production costs and state-of-the-art facilities, India is already pulling in global animation business. A report by Anderson Consulting pegs the Indian animation industry at $570 million in early 2005, with a growth rate of 30 percent annually in the next three years (p. 78).

In addition to outsourcing, the concept of coproduction is also beginning to take root. Most European countries have signed treaties whereby they can access each other's facilities and enjoy the most-favored-nation status. Moreover, a film, subject to a host of criteria, can avail of tax credits and grants that would bring down the financing costs. The United Kingdom and India were expected to sign a coproduction pact in 2005 (p. 78). These are clear indications of the transnationalization of the film industry as a market enterprise of global media producers who share class interests regardless of national and cultural differences.

Perhaps a more important benefit of globalization from the standpoint of humanity, rather than the narrow corporate interest in profit, is its potential for promoting an improved understanding and appreciation of world cultures. A new study, sponsored by the UCLA Ronald W. Burkle Center for International Relations, says growing Asian competition with the Hollywood film industry may not be a bad thing. Tom Plate, a professor at UCLA, noted the increasing Asianization of the film business could represent globalization at its most desirable. "Exposing a broader sector of the U.S. audience to divergent cultural and political perspectives could prove of enormous value. Rather than experiencing a fearsome and reductive 'clash of civilizations,' we would get a truly cosmopolitan world entertainment media (e.g., more movies might even show serious problems being solved without guns or bombs)," he says. Mass entertainment, concludes the study, "will not in itself be adequate to overcome inclinations toward hatred and violence. But it can help" (Plate 2002)—depending of course on who makes content, style, production, and distribution decisions.

REINVENTION AND REALIGNMENT

As we have seen, film industries in several Asian countries are going through a process of reinventing themselves to maintain their economic viability amidst the globalizing media culture of the West, especially the United States. These changes reflect, in part, claims of cultural dependency as well as the market model of Hollywood's well-established production formula for commercial success. At the Global Fusion 2004 conference in St. Louis in late October 2004, one media scholar cited the cultural dependency theory, or the cultural imperialism of the West, as the explanation for the changing South Korean film industry. In his paper, the scholar noted that as some Korean films are becoming huge commercial successes by incorporating Hollywood-style themes and production techniques, their appeal in America was on the rise, which the scholar interpreted as "reverse cultural imperialism."

Indeed, *cultural imperialism* or its academic variant called *cultural dependency theory* are terms often used by scholars in international and cross-cultural communication to explain negative influences of the West on the cultures and media industries of developing nations. Some have even suggested that cultural imperialism is slowly killing off indigenous cultures in some parts of the world. These are extreme reactions based on misinterpretations of phrases such as *cultural imperialism*. There is no doubt, as Robert Keohane and Joseph Nye, Jr. (1998), argue, the ideological and material success of a country make its culture and ideology attractive internationally, especially if the country also happens to be a large one that is dominant militarily and technologically. If this is how cultural imperialism is defined, then it is obvious that by its nature cultural imperialism works through the appeal of a culture since the culturally imperialist country is not forcing anyone to adopt its culture. Across the globe, academic books, research journals, news, and cultural products from the West are valued as sources of information and enjoyment even as people in developing countries continue to cherish and enjoy their own cultures. This cultural imperialism appears as a benign or welcome force rather than a harmful one—a characteristic of cultural hegemony or leadership based on consent rather than an enforced imposition (Artz 2000, 2003).

So when a country's people or its media *choose* to adopt what appear to be the features of Western culture, we have to presume they are doing so because some element of the so-called imperial culture must be necessary to accept to fulfill their needs. As we have said, cultural imperialism, in the contemporary world, works by appeal rather than by force. Singapore, for example, carries BBC World Service on one of its FM radio stations twenty-four hours a day because the economic and political elite of that country value the importance of the English language in international business and commerce and want its population to be fluent in English for its continued economic success. Indeed, countries around the world are pushing the teaching of English as a second language because English has become the language of choice around the world for a variety of economic and political reasons, including market globalization and its accompanying emphasis on individualism and consumerism.

On the other hand, Asian filmmakers have been pressured to adopt Hollywood's lowest-common-denominator production formula—predicated on the themes of sex, violence, alcohol and drug use—to regain commercial success for their films, whose earlier themes of mushy love stories and family dramas have lost much of their appeal to an audience with access to the titillating offerings of the West through globalized Hollywood and television. The commercial success of Asian films based on the Hollywood formula, such as India's *Jism* or Korea's *Shiri*, underscores the point that it is the appeal of the Hollywood profit-driven production formula rather than a coercive cultural imperialism that is influencing Asian film industries. This is consistent with and reinforces the elite-popular-specialized media evolution theory, mentioned earlier in this article, which says that media have to be packaged around a popular appeal in economically modernizing societies with expanding numbers of media consumers. But depressed movie industries in Asia are learning that they are most likely to succeed when they borrow not only the Hollywood formula of sex, violence, and drugs, but also its creativity, technique, editing, and distribution elements. The Japanese and Korean movie industries have done that most effectively, and Bollywood is beginning to do so. Of course, the development of this popular appeal does not arise independently from the populations of Asia, but is promoted to fit the needs of the political economy, shared ideology, and profit drive of the commercial film industries in each country and transnationally.

An equally important point to note here is that there would be a greater likelihood of crossover of commercially successful production formulas from East to West (rather than just from West to East) if the economic viability of Hollywood depended on that than the likelihood of a "reverse cultural imperialism." This is because cultural imperialism is predicated on the notion of the appeal of the culturally dominant to the less dominant, whereas commercially successful media production formulas move freely to fulfill economic needs of a particular social class. The popularity and profitability of Japanese-, South Korean-, and Hong Kong–inspired films in America in recent years illustrates this point. Coproduction agreements between film producers internationally and outsourcing of film-related work further indicate that we will see increasing interdependence among film industries around the world.

APPENDIX
MAIN ASIAN TELEVISION STATIONS

China

TV Stations in Mainland
China Central TV
Hunan TV
Dragon TV
Phoenix TV
News Corporation
China Sun TV
Viacom
Stellar-Megamedia
Net and TV
Beijing TV

TV Stations Hong Kong

V stations in Hong Kong
Star TV
Cable TV
Television Broadcasts Ltd. (TVB)
Asia Television Ltd. (ATV)
ITVHK

Japan

TVNET Japan
NTV—Nippon Television Network
TBS—Tokyo Broadcasting System
CX—Fuji TV

KTV—Kansai Telecasting
ANB—Asahi National Broadcasting
NBN—Nagoya TV
TX—Television Tokyo Channel

India

AASTHA TV (CMM)
AAJ TAK/Headlines Today
TV Today Network Ltd.
The Nation's Best News Channel
Animal Planet
Asianet
ATN
BBC
B4U Television Network India Pvt. Ltd.
Cable News International Inc.
CINE Channel (CCC)
Channel NewsAsia
Channel Guide Inida Ltd.
CNN/Cartoon Network/Pogo/Turner
    India Pvt. Ltd.
CVO Cable Video India Ltd.
CNBC India TV 18 India Ltd.
Channel [V] Star India Ltd.
Channel 7 Jagran TV Pvt. Ltd.
Care TV
Doordarshan
ETV Eenadu TV

ESPN Sports and Software India Pvt. Ltd.

ETC Networks Ltd.

Gemini TV Sun Network

HBO

Hungama TV UTV Ltd.

India TV Independent News Service Pvt. Ltd

Jaya TV

Jain TV

Kairali TV Malayalam Communications Ltd.

Lashkara/Gurjari Reminiscent Communications

MTV Music Television MTV India Pvt. Ltd.

Maharishi Veda Vision Maharishi Shiksha Santhan

MAA Television Networks Ltd.

National Geographic Channel Star India Ltd.

NDTV India, NDTV 24x7 New Delhi Television Ltd.

Nepal 1 TV Live India Pvt. Ltd.

Raj TV, Raj Digital Plus

Sony Set India Ltd.

SAB TV Shri Adhikari Brothers Television Network Ltd.

STAR (Star Plus, Star Movies, Star News, Star World, Channel [V], Star Gold, National Geographic Channel), STAR India Ltd.

Sun TV Network (Sun TV, Gemini TV, Udaya, Surya, Teja TV, Sun News, Udaya News, Sun Pictures)

Sanskar TV Sanskar Info. TV Pvt. Ltd.

The Splash Channel

Sahara One

Tara

Teja TV Sun Network

Ten Sports

Udaya TV Sun Network

Ushe TV Sun Network

Vijay TV Television Ltd.

Zee TV Television Network

Zoom

Indonesia

ANtv (Anteve)

Global TV (TVG)

Indosiar

Latvian

Metro TV

RCTI

SCTV

TPI

Trans TV

TVRI

TV 7

LEADING FILM COMPANIES AND PRODUCERS IN ASIA

India

Rajshi

Sahara One Motion Pictures

Red Chillies Entertainment

Shahrukh Khan

Yash Raj Films Pvt. Ltd

UTV Motion Pictures

Ritesh Sidhwani

Cinedreams Production

Future East (formerly Film Republic)

KAS Moviemakers

Locations Asia

Suresh Productions/Rama Naidu Studios

China

State Administration of Radio, Film, and Television

China Film Group Corporation

CITIC Media Group

Shanghai Film Group

Changchun Film Group

Huayi Brothers

Asian Union Film and Media
Beijing Forbidden City Film Co.
Pegasus and Taihe Entertainment International
Beijing Rosat Film and TV Production Co. Ltd.
Tanglong International Media Group
Shintoho Motion Picture Company

Japan

Trotter Productions
Dreamteam Productions
100 Meter Films
Monolith Films
Movie-Eye Entertainment Inc.
Winery Productions

Korea

CJ Entertainment
UniKorea
KN Entertainment
J&H Enterprise
HUB Entertainment
Film Ji
Cinema Janise
Eagle Pictures
Cinema Service
ChungMuRo Fund
CineWorld
HyunJin Cinema
Popcorn Film

REFERENCES

"American pop penetrates worldwide" (1998, October 25). *Washington Post*, p. A01.

Artz, L. (2000). *Cultural hegemony in the United States.* Thousand Oaks, Calif.: Sage.

———. (2003). "Globalization, media hegemony, and social class." In L. Artz and Y. Kamalipour (eds.), *The globalization of corporate media hegemony*, pp. 3–31. Albany: State University of New York.

Australian Film Commission (2005). "Number of films released in Australia and selected countries: 2000–2004." At www.afc.gov.au/gtp/acomprelease.html (accessed December 11, 2005).

Bhatt, M. (2004, November 4). "Is Bollywood facing 'creative death'?" *Financial Express.* At www.financialexpress.com/latest_full_story.php?content_id=73310 (accessed February 20, 2005).

Biggins, O. (2004). "Cultural imperialism and Thai women's portrayals in mass media." Paper presented at the International Conference on Revisiting Globalization and Communication in the 2000s, Bangkok, Thailand.

"Bollywood finds sex sells in prudish India" (2004, October 21). Reuters. At www.reuters.co.uk/newsPackageArticle.jhtml?type=topNewsandstoryID=606613andsection=news (accessed October 22, 2004).

"Bollywood turns on the steam" (2003). AFP news story. At www.smh.com.au/articles/2003/06/03/1054406189392.html?oneclick=true (accessed September 18, 2004).

"Bring out your dead" (2005, October 9). *South China Morning Post.* At http://web.lexis-nexis.com/universe/printdoc (accessed December 21, 2005).

Chan, V.H.C. (2004, July 1). "Asian pop: Korean movies." At http://sfgate.com/cgi-bin/article.cgi?file=/gate/archive/2004/07/01/korcine.DTL (accessed December 15, 2005).

Chopra, A. (2005, Nov. 13). "Hindi film gets the indie spirit (no dancing, please)." *New York Times.* At www.nytimes.com/2005/11/13/movies/13chop.html? pagewanted=print (accessed November 13, 2005).

"Deepti criticizes pelvic age" (1999, September 8). *The Tribune,* Chandigarh, India.

"Downtown torpedoes" (2004). Film review. At www.hkfilm.net/movrevs/ dtorp.htm (accessed September 18, 2004).

Feaster, F. (2002). "The Hollywoodization of John Woo." At http://atlanta.creative loafing.com/2002-06-12/flicks_interview.html (accessed September 15, 2004).

"The Hollywoodization of Filipino movies" (2003, July 21). *Philippine Daily Inquirer.* At www.inq7.net/ent/2003/jul/22/ent_20-1.htm (accessed August 10, 2004).

"The Hollywoodization of the Thai film industry" (2004, May 1). *Siam Chronicle.* At http://news.ncmonline.com/news/view_article.html?article_id=da8e904d552d 47bd00d734e27c13015a (accessed August 15, 2004).

JETRO (2005, May). "Japanese film industry." At www.jetro.go.jp/en/market/ trend/industrial/pdf/jem0505-2e.pdf (accessed December 15, 2005).

Jihong, W., and Kraus, R. (2002, Fall). "Hollywood and China as adversaries and allies." *Pacific Affairs.* At www.findarticles.com/p/articles/mi_qa3680/ is_200210/ai_n9090593# continue (accessed December 11, 2005).

Kagon, J. (2005, May 1). "The possibilities for the future of the Japanese film." *Journal of Japanese Trade and Industry.* At http://web.lexis-nexis.com/universe/ printdoc (accessed December 11, 2005).

Keohane, R. O., and Nye, Jr., J. S. (September/October 1998). "Power and interdependence in the information age." *Foreign Affairs* 77(5), pp. 81–94.

Klein, C. (2003, March 25). "The Asia factor in global Hollywood." At http://yale global.yale.edu/display.article?id=1242 (accessed September 15, 2004).

"Korean films" (2004). At www.wordiq.com/definition/Contemporary_culture _of_South_Korea (accessed September 24, 2004).

Larsen, D. (2005, February 6). "Deep into Asian remakes." *Dayton Daily News.* At http://web.lexis-nexis.com/universe/printdoc (accessed December 11, 2005).

Lowenstein, R., and Merrill, J. (1990). *Macromedia.* New York: Longman.

Mander, J. (1996). "The dark side of globalization: What the media are missing." *The Nation.* At www.escape.ca/~viking/global.html (accessed September 22, 2004).

McLuhan, M. (1967). *The medium is the massage: An inventory of effects.* New York: Random House.

Menon, P. (2003). "Bollywood undressed." At www.student.city.ac.uk/~ra831/ group8/printer/prashprint.htm (accessed September 12, 2004).

Mishra, P. (2004, February 28). "Hurray for Bollywood." *New York Times.* At www.imsc.res.in/~rahul/articles/nyt12 (accessed September 16, 2004).

Mohammadi, A. (1995). "Cultural imperialism and cultural identity." In J. Downing et al. (eds.), *Questioning the media: A critical introduction,* pp. 362–378. Thousand Oaks, Calif.: Sage.

"On the world's movie map" (August 15, 2005). *India Today,* New Delhi, India, pp. 74–78.

Paquet, D. (2000). "Genrebending in contemporary Korean cinema." At www.ko-reanfilm.org/genrebending.html (accessed September 8, 2004).

Pendakur, M. (2003). *Indian popular cinema*. Cresskill, N.J.: Hampton.

Perry, A. (2003, October 20). "Queen of Bollywood." *Time*, Asia edition. At www.time.com/time/asia/covers/501031027/story.html (accessed August 10, 2004).

Phelan, S. (2005, April 3). "The ring master." *Sunday Herald*. At http://web .lexis-nexis.com/universe/printdoc (accessed December 11, 2005).

Plate, T. (2002). "Hollywood faces new competition: World film industry is globalization at its best." At www.international.ucla.edu/article.asp?parentid=2059 (accessed September 9, 2004).

Schiller, H. (1969). *Mass communication and American empire*. Boston: Beacon Press.

"The sun rises again on Japanese cinema" (2004, November 29). *Philippine Daily Inquirer*. At http://web.lexis-nexis.com/universe/printdoc (accessed December 11, 2005).

"Tokyo on the Hudson" (2005, September 4). *New York Times*. At http://select .nytimes.com/gst/abstract.html?res=F60C12F93D550C778CDDA00894DD4044 82andincamp=archive:movies_filmography (accessed December 11, 2005).

Walker, A. (2004, September 23). "Asia's sweetheart." *South China Morning Post*. At http://web.lexis-nexis.com/universe/printdoc (accessed Dec. 11, 2005).

"Where are the storytellers?" (2003, April 4). *The Hindu*. At www.thehindu.com/ thehindu/fr/2003/04/04/stories/2003040400020100.htm (accessed Dec. 14, 2005).

3

Europe: Television in Transition

Jeanette Steemers

As a media market Europe is distinctive and complex because of its enormous cultural and linguistic diversity. It is not a cultural-linguistic market in the sense of sharing "similar languages as well as intertwined histories and overlapping cultural characteristics" (McAnany and Wilkinson 1996, p. 16). It is instead composed of many single-language markets of varying size, which are largely, but not wholly, identifiable with nation-states. There is, of course, some degree of historical and cultural overlap. And in the case of television, larger nations such as France, Germany, and Britain overshadow smaller same-language neighbors in respect to both production capability and overspill transmissions.

But historically the media developed along national lines. In the pretelevision era, press growth was informed by different traditions—exemplified by the laissez-faire approach of Britain, the interventionist and centralist position of France, a decentralized model in Germany, and the corporatist model in Sweden, (Humphreys 1996, pp. 63–64). In postwar Europe, ideological differences became starkly apparent with the largely unregulated press and public service broadcasting (PSB) monopolies in the West, and the state-controlled media in communist-led Eastern and Central Europe. With the incorporation since 2004 of ten new member states into the European Union (EU), including Hungary, Poland, the Czech Republic, Slovakia, and the smaller Baltic states, the Western market-oriented model has prevailed.

Within this context television provides an interesting point of departure because it increasingly transcends national boundaries in terms of ownership, operational practices, and audience experiences. Admittedly the vast majority of television channels in Europe are still targeted at and consumed by distinct national audiences, because of cultural and linguistic barriers. Pan-European channels, even those that have been localized (e.g., Music Television MTV, Cable Network News CNN, Cartoon Network, Discovery, National Geographic), do not attract large audiences (Chalaby 2002, p. 189; Bondebjerg 2004, p. 70). However, increases in the proliferation of globally distributed television formats and channels since the late 1990s underline the global interconnectedness and experience of television, driven by media policies and strategies that promote similar market practices and goals (Waisbord 2004, p. 359). As a result, European audiences now experience a range of similar television, in a process characterized by Robertson as *glocalization*—the global production of the local and the localization of the global in an attempt to appeal to differentiated local markets (1994, 1995).

From this perspective, global trends such as the challenge of technological innovation, the rise of global markets, deregulation, and more intense commercial competition provide a compelling rationale to consider recent developments in European television. This chapter identifies significant trends in the institutional development of television, the legal and regulatory context, new technologies, and the production and international circulation of European television programming. Throughout the focus is on the television institutions, policies, and industries of those European countries that are members of the EU including the postcommunist societies of Eastern and Central Europe. The survey is underpinned by two key trends: The first involves the transition from a heavily regulated television environment, guided by nationally focused social, cultural, and political objectives to one driven by economic and global imperatives, over which national governments have less influence. The second involves the potential technological transformation of television as a cultural form and social institution and its convergence through digitization with other media and information sources to create an interactive, information-based society.

THE RISE OF THE COMMERCIAL SECTOR

European television underwent dramatic change in the 1980s from a landscape characterized by heavy regulation and public service or state monopolies to an abundance of offerings in a less heavily regulated dual system of competing private and public television stations, in which commercial operators dominate. This abundance was made possible with changes in physical delivery, starting with cable and satellite distribution in the 1980s, and more recently with digital transmission, which rapidly expanded the number of available channels and opportunities for on-demand services and interactivity.

Among the 452 million people of the expanding European Union of twenty-five members, there are 176 million TV households (EAO 2004a, p. 32). At the end of 2003 approximately 98 million homes had access to cable and satellite television, although penetration levels vary enormously from 98 percent of TV households in the Netherlands to as low as 21 percent in Italy (EAO 2004a, p. 32). In the EU, 17.3 percent of households had access to digital television at the end of 2003, led by Britain (49.6 percent) (EAO 2004a, p. 35). By September 2005, 62 percent of British homes had digital television, comprising 5.5 million homes subscribing to the digital terrestrial service Freeview, and a further 7.3 million homes subscribing to Sky Digital (Reevell 2005). A further 770,000 homes subscribe to the PVR, SkyPlus (Dacey 2005). Almost 22 million households subscribed to digital satellite pay television at the end of 2003, led by Britain (6.9 million), France (3.99 million), Italy (2.4 million), Spain (1.79 million) and Germany (1.5 million) (EAO 2004a, p. 67).

This expansion in television services is partially explained by technology, but was also propelled by wider political interests who wished to see the marketization of media and communications. Marketization involves the privatization of public enterprises (such as the French public channel TF1 in 1986), the liberalization of previously closed markets, the reorientation of regulation to promote business interests, and the corporatization of public sector organizations in pursuit of commercial opportunities and organization (Murdock and Golding 2001, p. 114). As a result of these changes, television in Europe shifted from being a service designed to meet distinct political, social, and cultural objectives connected with citizenship, political pluralism, and the maintenance of national culture—to one that is more consumer-oriented as economic, global, and industrial priorities take hold (Iosifides, Steemers, and Wheeler 2005).

This transformation has raised a number of uncertainties. These include the challenge of funding original production in a fragmenting market, the future of public service television in a multichannel landscape, the possible emergence of a two-tier society with the growth of subscription services, and the consolidated power of a small number of large, vertically integrated and often multinational corporations that control content, distribution, and consumer access across different media and international markets as integrated businesses (see Murdock 2000; Steemers 1997).

Until the 1980s television in Western Europe was largely run by public service monopolies with the exceptions of Luxembourg, Britain, and Finland. In a first wave of commercialization between 1980 and 1988 private television was launched in Italy, France, and Germany. In a second phase from the late 1980s until the early 1990s, it was introduced into Spain, Portugal, Greece, Benelux, and Scandinavia. The reality of transnational satellite transmissions made it harder to justify regulatory regimes based on public service monopoly, and countries like Sweden and Germany legislated to allow commercial television rather than have it imposed from abroad. The third phase of channel expansion started in the late-1990s and is tied to digitization and an expansion of different media channels and services.

In Eastern and Central Europe, television was dominated by state television until the early 1990s, prior to transformation into public networks. According to Jakubowicz (2004a), all public networks in the region are in crisis because of a combination of small markets, poor organization, lack of funding, and the weakness of civil society (p. 63). At a time when public service broadcasting (PSB) is in doubt in Western Europe, PSB in Eastern and Central Europe has not had time to develop and lacks the "social embeddedness and the right democratic context in which to operate" (Jakubowicz 2004a, p. 53). Since the early 1990s private networks, often owned by foreign interests (HBO, SBS, CME, RTL), have become dominant.

Across Europe, then, there is more consumer choice. Yet the financial risk associated with television means that new developments such as digital pay television and multiplatform applications have tended to be dominated by established commercial players with deep pockets to absorb the early losses (see Bustamante 2004). At the first level there are a small number of European companies with channel/production interests in several countries. They include the Bertelsmann-owned Radiodiffusion-Télévision Luxembourg (RTL) Group, Vivendi Universal (owner of pay channel Canal Plus, which has established ventures with local players across Europe), and the Scandinavian Broadcasting System (SBS), which operates channels in Scandinavia, Benelux, and Eastern Europe. However, linguistic and cultural barriers, the practice of selling rights on a territorial basis, and the complicated variety of regulations that exist within different countries, restrict most television activities within national boundaries (Iosifides, Steemers, and Wheeler 2005, p. 88). This is the case for Fininvest in Italy, ITV and BSkyB in the UK, and until its insolvency in 2002, the Kirch Group in Germany. This has placed European players at a disadvantage with U.S. rivals, whose scale in the U.S. domestic market has encouraged them to launch a raft of American-owned, but localized, thematic channels across Europe including Cartoon Network, CNN, MTV, National Geographic, Discovery, and Nickelodeon.

However, the rise of new media applications and subscription services raises a number of problems for traditional advertising-funded commercial channels, which have seen audience shares decline. For example, in the week ending August 14, 2005, Britain's two highest-rating television channels, BBC 1 and ITV 1, hit their worst-ever shares, 21.4 percent and 18.5 percent respectively, because of competition from multichannel television (Rogers 2005, p. 1). A financial crisis in advertising post-2001 combined with overzealous attempts to become vertically integrated organizations through acquisitions and investment in digital television led to high-profile corporate failures and retrenchment. German conglomerate Kirch Media collapsed in 2002 having paid too much for sports and film rights to feed its failing Premiere digital pay-television package. Vivendi Universal was forced to divest itself of its American assets in 2003 and merge its U.S. entertainment arm with U.S. media conglomerate General Electric, after overexpansion. ITV in the UK and RTL were forced to retrench after a decline in advertising revenues, and in ITV's case, commence a disastrous foray into the digital terrestrial pay-television venture ITV Digital. The rise of PVRs (Personal Video Recorders), which allow consumers to edit out advertising, combined with a decline in mass audiences, and threatens the traditional economic model underpinning advertising-funded channels. Broadcasters such as ITV, Channel 4, and RTL have tried to stem the decline in audience share by launching new secondary channels. They are also looking at developing new revenue streams from online activities and mobile phone applications, above all to attract younger viewers (see Snoddy 2005).

THE FUTURE OF PUBLIC SERVICE TELEVISION

Alongside the recent problems of commercial television, the radical transformation from public service or state-dominated monopolies to a predominantly commercial model has undermined the political, social, and cultural justification for public service broadcasters. These now have to demonstrate more clearly what distinguishes them from their commercial rivals in order to justify public support. This has become a much more difficult undertaking amid accusations that public television is no longer sufficiently distinctive to merit public funding, even more so if there is a significant dependence on commercial revenues, as there is in many countries. Only Norway, Britain, and Sweden do not take advertising on their public television services.

Historically public service monopolies were justified on the technical grounds of insufficient frequencies to allow a multitude of suppliers. In Western Europe, political and social justifications were added, which reflected the mood for collective solutions, serving society as a forum in the interests of democracy (Dahlgren 2000, p. 25). This brought noncommercial purposes and values to the fore, and these have traditionally underpinned the justification for PSB. These purposes include the provision of a diverse range of content, including entertainment and information, a plurality of viewpoints, universal access regardless of income or geographical location, public accountability, impartiality, and the maintenance and support of national cultural identity. Traditionally a small number of generalist channels met these purposes with a mix of programming.

These noncommercial purposes provide the main justification for public service broadcasting (Graham 2000), but in practice the degree to which they have been met varies considerably. In some countries, such as France, Italy, and Greece, party political interference affected the implementation and effectiveness of public service television (Hibberd 2001; Papathanassopoulos 2004, p. 95; Smith 1998, p. 41). In others, reliance on commercial advertising revenues or the pursuit of commercial policies sits uneasily next to a commitment to a noncommercial public service ethos (see McKinsey 1999). For example, the emergence of the BBC's commercial subsidiary, BBC Worldwide, as Europe's largest exporter of television programs and a key partner in joint channel ventures with commercial partners, such as Discovery Communications Inc. and Flextech/Telewest, has attracted criticism that these activities go beyond the corporation's remit and undermine opportunities for other commercial enterprises.

In all countries the loss of monopoly led to changes in programming policy and schedules to retain audiences. In France, Spain, and Italy, where public television is partially funded by advertising, commercial competition in the 1980s led to an aggressive pursuit of ratings. This resulted in more emphasis on popular entertainment at the expense of information and cultural programming in order to retain audiences and attract advertising revenues (Humphreys 1996, p. 233; Sartori 1996, p. 156; Padovani and Tracey 2003). As a rule public broadcasters who have limited (ZDF and ARD in Germany) or no television advertising (the BBC in Britain and SVT in Sweden) have tended to maintain a more distinctive public service profile (McKinsey 1999).

Commercial competition represents one challenge to public service television. But technological change also begs the question of the degree to which publicly funded media should be allowed to participate in new media—particularly in a situation where television now forms just one element in a broader array of electronic media experiences. For larger, more affluent public broadcasters, such as the BBC in the UK and ARD and ZDF in Germany, digital channels and the new media are increasingly used to target different minority groups and interests, predicated on projections of changing audience expectations, habits, and tastes (see Born 2003, p. 794). For example, the BBC (CBBC and CBeebies) and ARD/ZDF (Kika), launched children's channels in the late 1990s as part of a portfolio approach, which also includes cultural and documentary channels and an Internet presence. However, this has led to conflict with commercial operators, who would prefer public service television's remit to be limited to a range of complementary minority activities in old media, which do not conflict with their commercial ambitions. For smaller public broadcasters with fewer financial resources, there are limited options to fund new services or technologies or invest in high-profile domestic content such as drama to retain audiences. As a consequence some public broadcasters in Portugal, Greece, Belgium, and Eastern Europe, have become increasingly marginalized (see Iosifides, Steemers, and Wheeler 2005; Jakubowicz 2004a).

Whatever strategy is taken, all public broadcasters have to tread the difficult line between balancing the need to be popular with the requirement to provide a distinctive and valuable alternative to commercial television (Syvertsen 2003, p. 170). If deemed too popular they run the risk of raising questions about public funding, but this is also the case if they air minority programming and alienate a large proportion of the public. They need to find a balance between providing innovative content, which commercial suppliers are unwilling or unable to provide, and also meeting the needs of the mass audience. They need to engage across platforms with a younger audience, which is increasingly unenamoured by PSB offerings. They also need to deal with proposals to top-slice public funding to finance alternative suppliers of public service programming, put public service content out to tender; or attempts to restrict the public service remit to a much narrower range of programming. For example, from 2008, Dutch public service content provision is likely to be restricted to three citizen-oriented functions—news, opinion-forming/public debate, and education/arts/culture, with entertainment permissible, but not a goal in itself (Anon 2005; Netherlands Scientific Council 2005).

THE LEGAL AND REGULATORY CONTEXT: NATIONAL APPROACHES AND PAN-EUROPEAN CONTEXTS

These ongoing changes in media and communications have forced regulators to deal with questions about what type of regulation is appropriate for a television landscape characterized by channel abundance, technological convergence, global media corporations, and the delivery of content to a range of platforms including computers and mobile phones, where content is not governed by media regulation. In the past the European television sector was highly regulated in respect of content, access, and ownership because of its opinion-forming power, a scarcity of frequencies, which did not allow a large number of competing channels, and the high costs of television, which mitigated against a plethora of players. Regulation was meant to ensure and encourage quality, cultural diversity, political pluralism, domestic production, and fair market access based on the assumption that the market alone would not deliver these goals. Regulation of ownership was deemed especially important for maintaining democratic debate, because it was and still is characterized by high levels of media and cross-media concentration stemming from the substantial costs of entering the marketplace (Iosifides 1997).

However, conscious of a rapidly expanding global communications market, national governments and the European Union have tried to promote international competitiveness, mindful of the fact that globalization and technological convergence are rendering sectoral control on a national basis much more difficult. Regulation has therefore been adjusted to reflect a lighter-touch approach that places more reliance on economic regulation in the form of competition law and self-regulation, rather than cultural policy (Syvertsen 2003, p. 169). Governments have accepted pro-market arguments about greater consumer choice and commercial freedom in the expectation of larger economic benefits and the expansion of the media and communications sector (Humphreys and Lang 1998, pp. 17–18).

First, on a practical level, satellite transmission made it more difficult to prevent commercial television being beamed into countries from outside national borders. Second, commercial media interests lobbied politicians to allow them to expand across sectors and develop new media technologies without the burden of restrictive legislation and ownership rules (Humphreys and Lang 1998; Iosifides, Steemers, and Wheeler 2005, p. 66). Concentration measures are mainly left to individual states, with the EU, which has endorsed media consolidation, scrutinizing mergers and acquisitions under competition law (see Wheeler 2004, p. 361).

The blurring of boundaries between television, computing, and telecommunications has also impacted regulatory initiatives, undermining sector-specific approaches based on the public good. As a result there has been regulatory convergence at an institutional level. Television is now increasingly regulated by the same bodies that are also responsible for other sectors in the media and telecommunications industry. For example, the UK regulatory body Ofcom (the Office of Telecommunications) is responsible for all sectors of the communications industry. Unified regulatory bodies have also been introduced in Italy and Finland.

Alongside national regulation, there is a European dimension heavily focused on international competitiveness, market liberalization, and harmonization. The liberalizing cornerstone of the EU's regulatory framework for the audiovisual industries was the *Television Without Frontiers*

(TWF) Directive in 1989, which is currently being revised to meet technological and economic developments (European Council 1989). This created a single integrated market, with common rules on issues such as advertising, sponsorship, and the protection of minors. In creating a single market, the EU sought to facilitate the unification of an undercapitalized European television industry in order to promote a more sustainable European television economy and develop a production infrastructure, which could compete with the United States (Wheeler 2004, p. 351). The single market was meant to bridge the gap between a few powerful broadcasters who control delivery and a much larger number of fragmented and undercapitalized production companies.

However, the EU's efforts at liberalization and harmonization are at odds with a more interventionist approach, rooted in cultural concerns about pluralism and cultural diversity. This approach is reflected in Article 4 of the TWF directive, which requires broadcasters "where practicable" and "by appropriate means" to reserve a majority of transmission time for European productions (excluding news, sports, advertising, teletext, and teleshopping). The imposition of quotas stemmed from concerns about the ability of Europe to support the production and circulation of European programming and apprehension about the Americanization of mass culture and television in particular. However, quotas were not particularly effective in either maximizing European program investment or stemming U.S. imports, because of elastic wording and widespread noncompliance (European Commission 2005; Levy 1999; Oliver and Ohlbaum 2003, p. 10). Quotas proved ineffective in stemming cheap U.S. imports, because the introduction of commercial channels in the 1980s created a demand for fiction that could not be satisfied by Europe's small and fragmented independent production sector (Dupagne and Waterman 1998, p. 216). However, quotas have fueled controversy on the international stage. The EU has had to defend these interventionist measures in multilateral WTO (World Trade Organization) negotiations on the GATS (General Agreement on Trade in Services), particularly against the United States, whose position has always been that television programs are commercially traded products like any other (see Thussu 2000, p. 180).

The EU's position on public service broadcasting has always been more ambiguous (see Jakubowicz 2004b). The Education and Culture Directorate has been supportive of PSB and pluralism, but there has been less support from the Competition and Information Society Directorates, which promote a market-oriented approach to the internal market and communications sector and tend to treat PSB as economic operators subject to normal constraints (Wheeler 2004, p. 353). With the transfer of audiovisual matters from Education and Culture to the Information Society and Media Directorate in 2005, the market-oriented approach is likely to continue. The Amsterdam Protocol, approved by member states in 1997, allows member states to determine the level and type of funding for public service broadcasting. However, since 2001, the European Commission has made the acceptance of mixed PSB funding systems (state subsidies and commercial funding) contingent on a precise definition of PSB, entrusted by law to one or more providers, and regulated by an appropriate authority (European Commission 2001). On a case-by-case basis, the EU has used these definitions to determine whether public funding is always necessary for the fulfillment of the public service mission, and whether the funding of PSB distorts the market and constitutes an abuse of state aid (European Commission 2001). Complaints have focused on the legality of new public service channels/services and mixed-funding arrangements. The European Commission has rejected several complaints by commercial broadcasters against the expansion of PSB into thematic channels, suggesting that dedicated children's (Kinderkanal, Germany), news (BBC News 24), and information (Phoenix, Germany) channels represent legitimate extensions of the public service remit, subject to proportionate funding (Jakubowicz 2004b, p. 168; Ward 2003). It has also rejected several complaints against mixed funding, but complaints about financial transparency and the use of public funding to support online developments remain a subject of future conflict with cases pending against the Netherlands, Germany, and Ireland.

THE CHALLENGE OF NEW TECHNOLOGIES

Alongside structural and legislative reforms, European television promises to change further with the digital revolution that permits content and services to be accessed on-demand via a number of different platforms, including broadband Internet and mobile phones, as well as digital cable, satellite, or terrestrial television (Carter 2005). In many European countries there are plans to switch off analogue television signals and migrate to digital transmission, removing the distinction between free-to-air channels and the multichannel universe. In Britain this will occur between 2008 and 2012. For some these changes herald the potential demise of traditional broadcast television based on conventional commissioning, linear broadcast schedules, and advertising sales and a shift toward demand-driven instead of supply-driven media. There are growing concerns within the television industry that broadcasters are set to lose control of distribution altogether with the entry of telecommunications and Internet players such as Yahoo! and Google, as consumers learn how to access television content directly in a consumer-driven landscape, notwithstanding fears about illegal downloads (Dignam and Robertson 2005, p. 2; Snoddy 2005).

In response larger European broadcasters are looking to extend "old-media linear networks" into online space by streaming content to mobile phones and enabling on-demand downloads (Dignam and Robertson 2005). These responses build on the broadcasters' current strengths, which include the harnessing of creative ideas, the ownership of key content rights, brand awareness, and their ability to deliver large audiences for certain types of content, such as sport and soaps (Bashford 2005, p. 19). Examples include the BBC's MyBBCPlayer, which launched in September 2005 as a trial. This allows the public to search for and download BBC programs that have been broadcast the week previously with plans to extend the service to live streams and other broadcasters' content (see White 2005). However, whatever concerns there may be about new forms of intermediation, rights continue to act as a barrier against such applications with rights-holders among the independent production community anxious to secure fair recompense for the multiple exploitation of their intellectual property.

Although much is being made of the potential of new technologies and digitization to change the experience of television, its structure, and competitive paradigm, the European reality may turn out to be slower and more uneven than intended. Digital television is available in most European markets. However, by the end of 2003, penetration varied greatly led by Britain (49 percent), Ireland (34 percent), Sweden (28 percent), and France (21 percent), but with less than 10 percent penetration in Austria, Belgium, Germany, Greece, Portugal, the Netherlands, and Central and Eastern Europe (EAO 2004a, p. 35). In the case of multichannel analogue television and later digital television, expansion has mainly focused on more television channels and the recycling of material rather than innovative interactive applications (apart from shopping), which have been slow to materialize and face competition from the Internet (Jensen 2005; Goodwin 2005, p. 176).

While the progress of digital pay television seems assured in larger markets with limited free-to-air competition and an early conversion to digital satellite transmission, such as Britain, there have been some high-profile failures and moves to consolidate as well. The high costs of programming, sports rights, marketing, and technical infrastructure mean that at most only one or two predominantly established players can coexist in each national market. They include News Corporation with its controlling stake in Britain's BSkyB and Italy's Sky Italia satellite platforms, Vivendi-Universal, and Liberty Media, a major provider of broadband communication and digital cable television across Europe. The German market has proved particularly resistant to subscription television because of the large number of advertising-supported services available in analogue cabled homes. In 2002 there were digital terrestrial pay-television failures in Spain (Quiero TV) and Britain (ITV Digital), because consumers were not convinced by the more limited choice of the terrestrial platforms compared to the greater number of services available on digital satellite television. The economic risks associated with competition in the market for digital pay television led to the merger of the Telepiù and Stream digital satellite packages in Italy as Sky Italia in 2003, and of Canal Satélite Digital and Via Digital in Spain in 2002. However, consolidation raises the regulatory challenges of bottlenecks and vertical integration. This occurs as key players start to control production and distribution chains through their domination of content, key sporting rights, delivery systems, and consumer access, to the exclusion of other operators and to the detriment of pluralism and the free flow of information (Steemers 1997, p. 67).

PRODUCTION TRENDS: EUROPEAN TELEVISION IN THE GLOBAL MARKETPLACE

It has already been shown how the European television landscape has changed radically within a remarkably short period in terms of institutions, regulatory frameworks, and technology, but content will be a key driver behind change. However, as a global television player, Europe is a serious underperformer—both in its ability to export programming and also in terms of the dominance of U.S. fiction when it comes to imports (see Buonanno 2000; Tunstall and Machin 1999). Most European countries import very little from each other and large amounts of fiction from the United States.

In 2002 European broadcasters spent an estimated EUR 2.25 billion on U.S. TV imports and a further EUR 3 billion on U.S. feature films (European Commission 2005, p. 54). Intra-European trade in films and television totaled EUR 1–1.5 billion (European Commission 2005, p. 54). With European television exports to the United States valued at only EUR 500 million, Europe was staring at a television programming trade deficit with the United States of EUR 1.75 billion (excluding film acquisitions) in 2002. Exports are dominated by Britain, which benefits from a shared language and cultural proximity with the United States, which is its largest market, accounting for 39 percent of British trade (PACT 2005). Intra-European trade is dominated by the larger nations of Britain, France, and

Germany, whose wealth and population size allow them to support higher levels of production.

The United States dominates the global trade in finished programs with an estimated 70 percent share by hours ahead of Britain (10 percent). Yet, domestic programming dominates mainstream free-to-air peak time schedules in Europe, because audiences prefer homegrown programming. Imports are estimated to have declined by 16 percent on these channels from 34 percent of airtime in 1996–1997 to 28 percent in 2003 (BTDA 2005, p. 4). This is because of increases in local production, which delivers larger audiences. However, acquisitions have ballooned on numerous secondary and subscription channels, which tend to recycle older material and U.S. imports.

Europe's poor trading position is affected by its culturally diverse nature, which does not lend itself to large-scale production or cross-cultural exchange. Unlike America, domestic markets are not large enough to recoup the costs of a $3 million per episode sitcom. As a consequence, in spite of audience preferences for local production, these are often ignored in favor of more cost-effective fiction imports—primarily from the United States. European buyers tend to prefer U.S. fiction featuring recognizable casts, settings, and storylines rather than European imports, which are deemed too culturally specific (Steemers 2004). There is only limited circulation of European drama within Europe because of a lack of cultural proximity (Straubhaar 2000) and the workings of cultural discount, where cultural differences pertaining to style, values, beliefs, institutions, and behavioral patterns limit the appeal of foreign programs (Hoskins and Mirus 1988, p. 500). European drama coproductions are rare and tend to focus on a narrow range of material based on historic figures and classic literary works, with little demand for contemporary drama, unless this is between same-language neighbors (Steemers 2005). In its 2003 survey of European drama coproduction, Eurofiction established that there were eighty-three inter-European coproduced titles and twenty-five coproduced titles with third countries (EAO 2004b, p. 81)—a decline of 39 percent from the previous year.

Audience preferences for locally originated material combined with globalization, are reflected in the expansion of the trade in entertainment formats, a trade in which Europe has emerged as an apparent leader (Fry 2000). In a more competitive fragmented marketplace these have proved a cost-effective way of filling schedules with local productions and for overcoming the cultural barriers to stock programming such as drama and sitcoms. They offer a practical route around quotas and cultural difference because they are "culturally specific but nationally neutral" (Waisbord 2004, p. 368). Smaller nations have also made a mark, and in one recent survey, the Netherlands accounted for 15 percent of trade in volume in 2003 behind Britain (45 percent) and the United States (20 percent) on the back of shows such as *Big Brother*, *Master Plan*, and *Test the Nation*, all owned by Endemol (BTDA 2005).

The rise in entertainment formats underlines the growing demand for locally originated programming and the trend toward the global dispersal of locally originated formats and concepts. In some cases European players have managed to achieve success in the highly competitive U.S. marketplace while lacking the control of distribution (channels) to make this success more permanent. However, formats are not a solution to Europe's trade deficit, because revenues are modest and only generate from 10 to 20 percent of the value of finished programs (BTDA 2005, p. 24). They have little residual value as reruns and are only really significant if owners can realize value from exerting control over production in key territories like the United States. The importance of local production is illustrated in a recent survey by the Format Recognition and Protection Association (Frapa) that placed European companies Endemol (EUR 1.5 billion), Fremantlemedia (EUR 982 million), the BBC (EUR 443 million), and Granada (EUR 373 million) as the most successful format companies worldwide in the three years prior to 2004. These are all large companies that can produce globally or circulate formats to their local affiliates or commercial partners (Waller 2005).

The key to expanding exports lies in strengthening the production sector and ensuring that producers retain their intellectual property rights. Independent producers across Europe point out that such rights retention is vital in enabling them to build an asset base to attract investment, diversify, and grow (see European Commission 2005, p. 167). Without this asset base they have been reliant on production revenues from broadcasters who typically retain control of domestic as well as secondary overseas and ancillary rights. In Britain the rights situation changed in 2004 with terrestrial broadcasters now only able to buy primary rights in the first instance. According to one report this has encouraged a "substantial cultural change" (BTDA 2005, p. 35), characterized by the emergence of "a cluster of outward-looking, more risk-positive companies with business models geared to production for the world market and to the maximization of the global value of TV-driven intellectual programme rights" (BTDA 2005, p. 6). This is reinforcing a premier division of "super-indies" that are attractive to investors (HIT Entertainment, RDF Media, Tiger Aspect, Celador, 19TV), more diversified, and exploiting key rights and brands globally, particularly formats. By contrast Germany's poor position in the formats market has been blamed on broadcasters securing a total buyout of rights, whereas the Netherlands' strong position has been attributed to producers' retention of rights (C21 2005).

With liberalization and audience fragmentation, we may be seeing a shift in the relationship between European broadcasters and producers toward a new paradigm for the global exploitation of content. This shift involves a greater role for a small tier of production companies whose efforts on the global stage are marked by specialization and a growing interest in marketing and producing programs and formats for national markets and platforms worldwide.

COMMERCIAL TELEVISION ON THE RISE

The European television market continues to undergo rapid change. First, the expansion of the European Union has increased the size of the single market, with further expansion imminent. Cable and satellite have encouraged new commercial opportunities, more television outlets, and a light-touch regulatory approach. Further changes are expected with the digitization of television and technological convergence between television and other platforms. Commercial television appears to be gaining the ascendancy in most markets. This and new technological developments have intensified the debate about public service television, whose future may be determined at a European level, as the European Union becomes more involved in decisions relating to competition law and the use of state funding, placing public service broadcasting under more pressure in respect of its funding, structures, and programming policies. Deregulation has promoted the television industries and market opportunities, but the priorities of liberalization sit uncomfortably next to the social and political priorities associated with pluralism and diversity.

A combination of private and publicly owned channels is likely to continue in the medium term. At the same time there are visible trends toward increased niche provision, a growth in subscription funding, a decline in public funding, and an increase in consolidated cross-media ownership. Digital television and the delivery of television by other means (mobile telephony, broadband) are happening, but their spread continues to be uneven. Digital take-up has been variable, with high-profile failures. One prominent weakness is Europe's inability to produce sufficient content. The European production industry has been too fragmented to fill the growing demand for programming, making Europe vulnerable to inroads by overseas suppliers, foremost America. Formats have been an international success story for a small number of European companies, but without control of distribution this success may prove temporary.

APPENDIX

Television and Press Outlets in the European Union

Country	Public Broadcasters Channels	Principal Commercial Television Channels	Principal Newspapers
Austria	Österreichischer Rundfunk und Fernsehen (ORF) ORF-1 ORF-2		Neue Kronen-Zeitung Kurier Kleine Zeitung Die Presse
Belgium * Wallonia)	Radio-Télévision Belge de la Communauté Française (RTBF) La Une La Deux	RTL-TVI Club RTL Canal Plus Belgique (pay-TV) Le Bouquet (package)	Rossel (Le Soire, La Meuse, La Lanterne, La Nouvelle Gazette) Mediabel (La Libre Belgique, La Derniere Heure, L'Avenir)
Belgium * Flanders	Vlaamse Radio en Televisieomroep (VRT) TV-1 Ketnet/Canvas	VTM Kanaal 2 VT-4 Canal Plus Televisie	Flanders VUM De Standaard Het Niewsblad Het Volk De Gentenaar De Persgroup Het Laatse Nieuws De Morgen
Cyprus	RIK 1 RIK 2	SIGMA TV Kanali	O Phileleftheros Cyprus Weekly Ergatiko Vima
Czech Republic	CT—Ceska Televize CT 1 CT 2 CT 24 (news)	Nova TV Prima	Mladá fronta Dnes Právo Blesk Super
Denmark	Danmarks Radio (DR) DR1 DR2 TV-2 TV-2 Zulu	TV-3 (satellite) TV Danmark (terrestrial) Canal Digital (satellite) Viasat (satellite)	Morgenavisen Jyllands-Posten Berlingske Tidende Politiken BT Ekstra Bladet
Estonia	Eesti Televisioon (ETV)	TV3 Kanal 2	SL Ohtuleht Eesti Ekspress Eesti Päevaleht
Finland	Yleisradio (YLE) TV-1 TV-2	MTV 3 Channel Four (Nelonen)	Helsingen Sanomat Ilta-Sanomat Aamulehti Iltalehti Turun Sanomat

Country	Public Broadcasters Channels	Principal Commercial Television Channels	Principal Newspapers
France	France-Télévision France 2 France 3 France 5 Arte	TF1 M6 Canal Plus (pay-TV)	*L'Equipe* *Le Monde* *Le Parisien* *Le Figaro* *Libération* *Les Echos*
Germany	Zweites Deutsches Fernsehen (ZDF) ZDF Arbeitsgemeinshaft der Rundfunkanstalten Deutschlands (ARD) ARD Third Channels—ARD 3 ARD/ZDF Joint 3SAT KiKa (children's) Phoenix (documentary) Arte (arts/culture)	ProSiebenSat.1 Media AG Sat. 1 ProSieben Kabel 1 N24 Premiere (pay-TV package) RTL RTL II SuperRTL Vox	*Bild-Zeitung* *Süddeutsche Zeitung* *Frankfurter* *Allgemeine Zeitung* *Die Welt*
Greece	Elliniki Radiofonia Teleorasis (ERT) ET-1 NET ET-3 (Thessaloniki)	Mega Channel Antenna Alpha TV Star Channel Nova (digital package)	*Ta Nea* *Eleftherotypia* *Ethnos* *To Vima*
Hungary	Magyar Televizio M1 M2	TV2 RTL Klub TV3	*Metro* *Blikk* *Népszabadság* *Szines Mai Lap*
Ireland	Radio Telefís Eireann (RTE) RTE-1 Network 2 Telefís na Gaeilge (TG4)	TV3	*Irish Independent* *Irish Times* *Star*
Italy	Radiotelevisione Italiana (RAI) Rai Uno Rai Due Rai Tre	RTI/Mediaset Canale 5 Rete 4 Italia 1 Sky Italia (digital satellite package)	*Il Corriere della Sera* *La Repubblica* *Il Sole24ore* *La Stampa*
Latvia	LTV LTV1 LTV 2	LNT TV3 TV Riga PBK	*Diena* *Neatkariga Rita Avize* *Subbota*

Country	Public Broadcasters Channels	Principal Commercial Television Channels	Principal Newspapers
Lithuania	LNRT LTV LNK	Tele-3/TV3 Baltijos TV	*Lietuvos Rutas* *Kauno Diena* *Respublika*
Luxembourg	—	RTL Group Radio Television Letzebuerg	*Lusemburger wort* *Tageblatt*
Malta	TVM	Super One TV Net TV	
Netherlands	Nederlandse Omroep Stichting (NOS) Nederland 1 Nederland 2 Nederland 3	RTL RTL4 RTL 5 Yorin SBS 6 V-8 Net 5	*De Telegraaf* *Volkskrant* *Algemeen Dagblad* *NRC Handelsblad*
Poland	Telewizja Polska (TVP) TVP 1 TVP 2 TVP 3	Polsat TVN 7 Canal Plus (pay-TV)	*Gazeta Wyborcza* *Super Expres* *Rzeczpospolita* *Polityka*
Portugal	Rádiotelevisão Portuguesa (RTP) RTP-1 RTP-2	SIC TV1	*Público* *Diário de Notícias* *Expresso* *Jornal de Notícias* *Correio da Manhã*
Slovak Republic	STV STV 1 STV 2	TV Markiza JOJ TV	*Novy Cas* *Pravda* *Sme*
Slovenia	RTVSlo TVS1 TVS2	CME —Pop TV —Kanal A	*Slovenske novice* *Delo* *Vecer* *Dnevnik*
Spain	Televisíon Española (TVE) La Primera (1956) La 2 (1965) Regional TV Stations (various)	Telecinco Antena 3 Canal Plus España Digital +	*El Pais* *El Mundo* *ABC*
Sweden	Sveriges Television (SVT) SVT-1 SVT-2	TV-4 (terrestrial) TV3 (satellite) Kanal 5 (satellite)	*Aftonbladet* *Dagens Nyheter* *Expressen*

Country	Public Broadcasters Channels	Principal Commercial Television Channels	Principal Newspapers
United Kingdom	British Broadcasting Corporation (BBC) BBC1 BC2 BBC Digital Channels BBC 3 BBC 4 BBC News 24 BBC Parliament CBeebies (preschool children) CBBC (children)	ITV Channel 4 Channel 5 BSkyB (digital satellite package)	*The Sun* *Mirror* *Daily Mail* *Daily Express* *Daily Telegraph* *Times* *Guardian* *Financial Times* *Independent*

Sources: M. Kelly, G. Mazzoleni, D. McQuail (eds.), *The Media in Europe*, 3rd ed., Sage: 2004; *European Audiovisual Yearbook*, European Audiovisual Observatory, Strasbourg: 2004; *Willings Press Guide* 2005.

REFERENCES

Anon (2005, June 2). "Public broadcasting's future the subject of political debate." *Hilversummary*, pp. 1–3.

Bashford, S. (2005, August 19). "The magic of touch." *Broadcast*, p. 19.

Bondebjerg, I. (2004). "Television and the European Union." In J. Sinclair and G. Turner (eds.), *Contemporary world television*, pp. 67–71. London: British Film Institute.

Born, G. (2003). "Strategy, positioning and projection in digital television: Channel Four and the commercialization of public service broadcasting in the UK." *Media Culture and Society* 25(6), pp. 773–799.

BTDA: British Television Distributors Association (2005). *Rights of Passage. British Television in the Global Market*. London: UK Trade and Investment.

Buonanno, M., ed. (2000). *Continuity and Change*. Luton: University of Luton.

Bustamante, E. (2004). "Cultural industries in the digital age: Some provisional conclusions." *Media Culture and Society* 26(6), pp. 803–820.

C21 (2005). "Germans find format report tough reading." At http://www.c21media .net/features/detail.asp?area=2andarticle=24704 (accessed May 10, 2005).

Carter, M. (2005, August 19). "Why broadband is redefining TV." *Broadcast*, pp. 16–17.

Chalaby, J. (2002). "Transnational television in Europe: The role of Pan-European channels." *European Journal of Communication* 17(2), pp. 183–203.

Dacey, R. (2005, July 22). "What do *Playboy* and Andy Duncan have in common?" *Broadcast*, pp. 22–23.

Dahlgren, P. (2000). "Key trends in European television." In J. Wieten, G. Murdock, and P. Dahlgren (eds.), *Television across Europe*, pp. 23–34. London: Sage.

Dignam, C., and Robertson, C. (2005, August 19). "Content is still king." *Broadcast*, p. 2.

—— (2005, September 23). "Squaring up to television's future." *Broadcast*, pp. 6–7.

Dupagne, M., and Waterman, D. (1998). "Determinants of US television fiction imports in Western Europe." *Journal of Broadcasting and Electronic Media* 42(2), pp. 208–220.

EAO: European Audiovisual Observatory (2004a). *2004 yearbook, vol. 2.* Strasbourg: European Audiovisual Observatory.

—— (2004b). *2004 yearbook, vol. 5.* Strasbourg: European Audiovisual Observatory.

European Commission (2001, November 15). "Communication from the commission on the application of state aid rules to public service broadcasting." *Official Journal of the European Commission*, C 320/5, pp. 5–11.

—— (2005, May 24). *Impact study of measures (community and national) concerning the promotion of distribution and production of TV programs provided for under Article 25 (a) of the TV Without Frontiers Directive. Final Report.* Prepared by David Graham and Associates for The Audiovisual Media and Internet Unit, Directorate-General Information Society and Media, European Commission.

European Council (1989). *Council directive 89/552/EEC of 3 October 1989 on the coordination of certain provisions laid down by law, regulation or administrative action in member states concerning the pursuit of television broadcasting activities.* Brussels: European Council.

Fry, A. (2000, September 25). "Europe secure as leader of reality programming." *Variety*, pp. M4–M8.

Goodwin, P. (2005). "Never mind the policy, feel the growth." In A. Brown and R. G. Picard (eds.), *Digital terrestrial television in Europe*, pp. 151–181. Mahwah, N.J.: Lawrence Erlbaum.

Graham, A. (2000). "Public policy issues for UK broadcasting." In S. Barnett et al. (eds.), *E-Britannia: The communications revolution*, pp. 93–108. Luton: University of Luton.

Hibberd, M. (2001). "The reform of public service broadcasting in Italy." *Media, Culture and Society* 23(2), pp. 233–257.

Hoskins, C., and Mirus, R. (1988). "Reasons for the US dominance of international trade in television programs." *Media, Culture and Society* 10(4), pp. 499–515.

Humphreys, P. J. (1996). *Mass media and media policy in Western Europe.* Manchester: Manchester University.

Humphreys, P. J., and Lang, M. (1998). "Digital television between the economy and pluralism." In J. Steemers (ed.), *Changing channels: The prospects for television in a digital world*, pp. 9–35. Luton: University of Luton.

Iosifides, P. (1997). "Pluralism and media concentration policy in the European Union." *Javnost/The Public* 4(1), pp. 85–104.

Iosifidis, P., Steemers, J., and Wheeler, M. (2005). *European television industries.* London: British Film Institute.

Jakubowicz, K. (2004a). "Ideas in our heads: Introduction of PSB as part of media system change in Central and Eastern Europe." *European Journal of Communication* 19(1), pp. 53–74.

—— (2004b). "A square peg in a round hole: The European Union's policy on public service broadcasting." *Journal of Media Practice* 4(3), pp. 155–175 .

Jensen, J. (2005). "Interactive content, applications and services." In A. Brown and R. G. Picard (eds.), *Digital terrestrial television in Europe*, pp. 101–132. Mahwah, N.J.: Lawrence Erlbaum.

Levy, D. (1999). *Europe's digital revolution: Broadcasting regulation, the EU and the nation state*. London: Routledge.

McAnany, E. G., and Wilkinson, K. T. (1996). *Mass media and free trade*. Austin: University of Texas.

McKinsey (1999). *Public service broadcasting around the world: A McKinsey Report for the BBC*. January. At www.bbc.co.uk/info/bbc/pdf/McKinsey.pdf (accessed December 3, 2000).

Murdock, G. (2000). "Digital futures: European television in the age of convergence." In J. Wieten, G. Murdock, and P. Dahlgren (eds.), *Television across Europe*, pp. 35–57. London: Sage.

Murdock, G., and Golding, P. (2001). "Digital possibilities, market realities: The contradictions of communications convergence." In L. Panitch and C. Leys (eds.), *Socialist Register 2002*, pp. 111–130. London: Merlin.

Netherlands Scientific Council (2005). "Focus on functions: Challenges for a sustainable media policy, a summary of report 7 from the Netherlands Scientific Council for government policy." At http://www.wrr.nl/pdfdocumenten/r71se .pdf (accessed September 20, 2005).

Oliver and Ohlbaum Associates (2003). *UK television content in the digital age, sustaining the UK's TV content creation sector in the globalised 21st century: The role and importance of the BBC*. London: BBC.

PACT: Producers Alliance for Cinema and Television (2005). *2004 UK TV export revenue total nears $1bn*. London: PACT.

Padovani, C., and Tracey, M. (2003). "Report on the condition of public service broadcasting." *Television and New Media* 4(2), pp. 311–353.

Papathanassopoulos, S. (2004). "Greece." In M. Kelly, G. Mazzoleni, and D. McQuail (eds.), *The Media in Europe*, pp. 91–102. London: Sage.

Reevell, P. (2005, July 13). "How low will they go?" *Broadcast*, p. 13.

Robertson, R. (1994). "Globalization or glocalization?" *Journal of International Communications* 1(1), pp. 33–52.

––––– (1995). "Glocalization: Time-space and homogeneity-heterogeneity." In M. Featherstone, S. Lash, and R. Robertson (eds.), *Global Modernities*, pp. 33–44. London: Sage.

Rogers, J. (2005, August 19). "BBC1 and ITV1 hit worst ever share." *Broadcast*, p. 1.

Sartori, C. (1996). "The media in Italy." In A. Weymouth and B. Lamizet (eds.) *Markets and Myths*, pp. 134–172. London: Longman.

Smith, A. (1998). "Television as a public service medium." In A. Smith (ed.), *Television: An international history*, pp. 38–54. 2nd ed. Oxford: Oxford University.

Snoddy, R. (2005, September 16). "Invasion of the audience snatchers." *Broadcast*, pp. 20–21.

Steemers, J. (1997). "Broadcasting is dead: Long live digital choice." *Convergence* 3(1), pp. 51–71.

––––– (2004). *Selling television: British television in the global marketplace*. London: British Film Institute.

—— (2005, May) "No longer 'the best in the world': The challenge of exporting British television drama." *Media International Australia*, pp. 33–47.

Straubhaar, J. (2000). "Culture, language and social class in the globalization of television." In G. Wang, J. Servaes, and A. Goonasekera (eds.), *The new communications landscape*, pp. 199–224. London: Routledge.

Syvertsen, T. (2003). "Challenges to public television in the era of convergence and commercialization." *Television and New Media* 4(2), pp. 155–175.

Thussu, D. (2000). *International Communication: Continuity and change*. London: Arnold.

Tunstall, J., and Machin, D. (1999). *The Anglo-American media connection*. Oxford: Oxford University.

Waisbord, S. (2004). "McTV: Understanding the global popularity of television formats." *Television and New Media* 5(4), pp. 359–383.

Waller, E. (2005). "TV formats business at war." At http://www.c21media.net/features/detail.asp?area=2andarticle=24466 (accessed June 15, 2005).

Ward, D. (2003). "State aid or band-aid? An evaluation of the European Commission's approach to public service broadcasting." *Media, Culture and Society* 25(2), pp. 233–250.

Wheeler, M. (2004). "Supranational regulation: Television and the European Union." *European Journal of Communication* 19(3), pp. 349–369.

White, G. (2005, September 16). "The BBC's next techno-revolution." *Broadcast*, pp. 38–39.

4

The Middle East:
Transnational Arab Television

Marwan M. Kraidy and Joe F. Khalil

The Arab television industry is undergoing rapid transformations, the
nature and scope of which warrant an evaluation. A balanced analysis
is needed at a time when Arab mass media are the subject of intense interest from politicians, strategists, and academics in the Middle East, Europe, and North America within the highly politicized context of Middle
East governance, Arab-Western relations, and terrorism. To that end, this
chapter provides a general introduction to the Arab television industry,
establishing historical milestones and providing a broad survey of the
technological and politico-economic factors shaping contemporary Arab
television. We identify and analyze established and emerging trends in
the industry, including (1) the rise of regionalization, (2) the emergence of
niche media markets, (3) the birth of multiplatform "networks," and (4)
dominant genres like talk shows, reality television, and music video
"clips"—all of which advance the privatized corporate media model and
indicate the absence of public service broadcasting. The conclusion will
synthesize our findings and set some parameters for research on Arab television in the coming decade, with the caveat that in the fluid Arab television industry landscape, current patterns may change in the near future.
The appendixes present vital information about the industry intended to
help the reader to contextualize our analysis.

ARAB SATELLITE TELEVISION AND REGIONALIZATION

During the last fifteen years, Arab television experienced two radical
changes, moving at the same time from national systems to Pan-Arab

broadcasting and from government to private ownership. The significance of this twofold transformation can only be grasped when we consider Arab television history. Until the 1990s, private ownership of television in Iraq, Morocco, and most notably Lebanon was exceptional in a region where states owned and operated mass media systems believed to be essential for national cohesion and development (Kraidy 1998b). The most durable trend in private ownership is found in Lebanon, where the 1975–1990 war eroded state power and opened the floodgates for private— what Boyd (1991) calls "unofficial"—broadcasting, inaugurated in 1985 by the Lebanese Broadcasting Corporation (LBC) launched by the Christian militia Lebanese Forces. Competing militias followed suit, creating a wave of private television stations in the 1980s and 1990s, culminating in more than fifty television stations in 1995 (Kraidy 1998b).

In August 1990, after Iraqi forces invaded the neighboring country of Kuwait and the United States responded with a UN–sanctioned invasion of Iraq, Arab audiences turned to foreign news outlets for information. Notably, Saudi viewers, whose government waited three days before disclosing the invasion of a neighboring country (Kuwait) by another neighboring country (Iraq), turned en masse to CNN. Arab businessmen and politicians saw the popularity of transnational broadcasting and accelerated plans to launch Arab satellite channels (Kraidy 2002). The Middle East Broadcasting Corporation (MBC) was launched in London in 1991 by Walid Al-Ibrahimi, Saudi entrepreneur and son-in-law of King Fahd Bin Abdel Aziz. The state-owned Egypt Satellite Channel opened in the same year. They were followed by Arab Radio and Television (ART) in 1993, and Orbit Satellite Television and Radio Network in 1994, and in 1996 by the Lebanese Broadcasting Corporation (The Lebanese Satellite Channel) and Future Television (see Kraidy 1998a, for more on the Lebanese satellite channels). In 2005 there are more than one hundred Arab channels.

The 1991 Gulf War precipitated the creation of an industry whose technical and political bases had been established over the previous three decades. Arab information ministers, meeting in 1967, discussed the creation of a satellite network as a framework for the Arab League's social and cultural activities (Overview 1997), and two years later the Arab States Broadcasting Union (ASBU) was formed (Boyd 1999). At that time, there was political tension between Saudi Arabia and Egypt, and since Egypt led the establishment of the ASBU, Saudi Arabia did not join until 1974. Saudi Arabia and Egypt have historically been the two dominant Arab powers, and Saudi-Egyptian relations at that period were fraught with rivalry due to Egyptian social republicanism clashing with Saudi royalism, in addition to their sitting on opposite sides for a good part of the Cold War. Saudi Arabia took a leadership role in plans for the Arab satellite organization, ARABSAT, which was established in April 1976 as an organization affiliated with the Arab League (Overview 1997). Oil-rich Saudi Arabia bankrolled ARABSAT and its capitol, Riyadh, housed its headquarters. First-generation satellites ARABSAT 1-A and 1-B were launched in the 1980s and switched off in the early 1990s ("Satellite generations" 2002). Initially their use was restricted to official state channels in addition to Pan-Arab events, which explains why many private Arab broadcasters like ART, LBC, and Orbit used Telespazio's facilities in Italy for some time. ARABSAT launched its second-generation, geostationary, high-power satellites 2-A and 2SAT-B, carrying a total of thirty-four active transponders in 1996 (ARABSAT 1997). ARABSAT 3-A satellite was launched in February 1999, a powerful third generation covering all Arab countries, most of Europe, and a good part of Africa (see Amin and Boyd 1994; Kraidy 2002, for detailed discussions of this issue). Later, Arab television channels were able to take advantage of other satellites: First, was NILESAT 101, launched in 1998, which provided relatively affordable satellite space previously available only to national broadcasters via ARABSAT. NILESAT 101's immediate success with around one hundred channels prompted the launch of NILESAT 102 bringing the total used channels to around 240. NILESAT offered competitive prices to attract private channels broadcasting to the Arab World from Europe and to provide incentives for start-up channels. European satellites such as HOTBIRD are available, but fees are more costly than NILESAT's.

The emergence of satellite technology, the political fallout from the U.S. military occupation of Iraq, and economic considerations, led to the regionalization of Arab television. The Arabic language common to two hundred million viewers from Morocco to Iraq and a few dominant issues such as the Arab-Israeli conflict and the U.S. occupation of Iraq serve as a glue to this transnational audience. In news, this has led to the "anywhere but here" coverage phenomenon, where each channel takes the liberty to criticize all countries and policies except the country in which that channel is based or which finances its operations, and to a focus on transnational issues to the detriment of local and national issues. In entertainment, this has led to a real regionalization of Arabic song and the video "clips" industry, and to the integration, in reality television shows, for example, of participants from throughout the Arab world. Regionalization is also compatible with globalization in that it promotes industry practices that conform to the media market model (Artz 2003), including vertical integration, format-based production, and a transient and transnational workforce concentrated in Beirut, Cairo, and Dubai. These issues are discussed in detail in the following section of this chapter.

FROM REGIONALIZATION TO NICHE MARKETS

As we previously mentioned, the regionalization of Arab media was both a result of and a contributing factor to a convergence of technological and policy trends. Technologically, the advent of NILESAT created competition with ARABSAT, providing additional space for satellite transmission and reducing costs for broadcasters throughout the Middle Eastern and North African regions that fall under the footprint of both satellites. Beyond these technological advancements, policy developments were crucial in promoting and facilitating regionalization. First, most Arab governments relaxed policies initially designed to ban or control the spread of satellite dishes, and even where repressive official policies are maintained, laws are rarely enforced. Second, countries like the United Arab Emirates, Egypt, and Jordan established "free-media zones" with tax incentives and liberal labor regulations that enabled the pooling of resources and consolidation of talent. The Dubai Media City, the indisputable leader in this regard, now hosts dozens of regional and global corporate giants in broadcasting, information technology, advertising, and publishing. In addition, there are "unofficial free-media zones" in countries such as Lebanon and to a lesser extent Morocco, where educational, cultural, and business traditions promote media production.

The new satellite channels attempted at first to replace terrestrial channels with a mix of news and entertainment. The pioneer in this "general format" category was the aforementioned Middle East Broadcasting Center (MBC), which was in short time followed by others such as the Lebanese Broadcasting Corporation's satellite channel, the Lebanon-based Future Television, and to a lesser extent the Egyptian Dream TV. With news, each presented its owners' distinct political viewpoint, which differentiated these channels' newscasts from the "court news" style of official government television channels, whose newscasts lingered on the political and social activities of the countries' leaders. The new channels occasionally featured political dissidents, who broached sensitive topics that were never discussed on official television, thus raising the ceiling for political speech in the Arab region. At the same time, these same channels presented a new style of entertainment programs, characterized by high production values, a level of sensuality, and narrative dynamism that is more akin to the U.S. commercial network style than to the television productions of the developing world and even Europe.

Initially successful, these general mixed-format channels soon faced fierce competition from satellite pay-services. Pay-television entities such as Arab Radio and Television (ART), Orbit, and Showtime were interested in cultivating a niche audience willing to pay a subscription fee. It was just a matter of time before the market for generalist channels became saturated and new free-to-air broadcasters would have to move to a niche market strategy with audience segmentation. These developments made channels like MBC unsustainable and compelled them to reexamine their strategies at a time when niche strategy was becoming an increasingly viable option. Industry developments pushing for specialization and audience segmentation included the availability of unprecedented satellite space offered with financial incentives to broadcasters, the presence of production centers and free-media zones with proliferating production abilities, and the influence of the advertising industry, whose barons were interested in lowering the cost of advertisements on generalist channels by encouraging competition from specialized broadcasters.

Thematic channels were thus launched with the promise of offering specific audiences to advertisers. These broadcasters fell under two broad categories: news and entertainment; and within each category, competition has grown quantitatively and qualitatively. The success of the now-famous Qatari network, Al-Jazeera, and its editorial policy was soon followed by the Saudi-financed, Dubai-based Al-Arabyia, in addition to smaller 24-hour news channels, including the Syrian-owned Arab News Network (ANN), and more recently the Lebanese-based, London-registered, and Gulf-financed Arabic News Broadcast (ANB), and the U.S. government–sponsored Al-Hurra from a Virginia suburb of Washington, D.C. Continued competition for advertisers and audiences paved the way for yet another subdivision within the news sector, such as business news, travel news, and real estate news. For example, CNBC Arabia, a franchise of CNBC, is an Arabic-language financial news network based in the Dubai Media City. The trend toward specialization is also evident in entertainment channels, broadly defined as non-news channels. At the forefront are music channels displaying music videos 'round the clock, including the Egyptian Melody Hits, the Saudi-owned, Lebanon-based Rotana, with a pop music channel called Rotana Musica, and Rotana Tarab, specializing in classic Arab songs. Some of the music channels are on a solid economic footing because they market consumer commodities such as video requests, Web downloads, and live dedications using Short Messaging System (SMS) and Multimedia Messaging System (MMS). Text and multimedia messaging has become a major source of income for Arab satellite television channels. Many journalists speculate that some programs derive higher revenues from viewers' messaging than from advertisements, and telecommunications companies get a cut from the billings. Satellite television and mobile telecommunications executives are tight-lipped about figures.

Music channels also receive a boost from singing-and-performance reality television shows such as *Superstar* and *Star Academy*. Other forms of entertainment channels include those dedicated to Western entertainment, mostly U.S. situation comedies, dramatic series, and game shows, Arab movies and series, and lifestyle channels. Both Dubai Television's sister channel, One TV, and MBC 4 are dedicated to shows from the United States, United Kingdom, and Australia, broadcast with Arabic subtitles. Channels like Heya (She) TV or Nile Family feature shows about fashion, cooking, and home styling for a predominantly female audience.

Also on Arab airwaves are channels that cannot be described merely with the *news* or *entertainment* rubrics. These include religious channels such as the Saudi Iqraa and the televangelist Nour Sat. Shopping channels are another growth area of television programming available on dedicated satellite channels. Examples are Tamima TV broadcasting from Egypt and Thane International's Thane-Express Shop, which targets the Arab world from London. Finally, channels dedicated to fostering national identities by serving expatriate communities include the Persian Entertainment Network broadcasting Iranian music and entertainment and Middle East Television, which broadcasts in Malay, Hindi, and Tamil for expatriate laborers in the Gulf Cooperation Council countries. The growth of thematic channels has not obliterated general satellite channels. Rather, as the next section explores, the Arab media industry is now witnessing the rise of multiplatform television "networks."

THE ADVENT OF MULTIPLATFORM "NETWORKS"

The designation *networks* here has a different meaning than in the United States. We use it to refer to companies that develop multiple channels under the same name to cater to multiple niche audiences. While newcomers were expanding the satellite television environment, the well-established Arab satellite television channels were devising new strategies to consolidate their stand, maintain their audience, and display their products. This movement can be compared to the CNN, MTV, and NBC expansions in the 1990s when these channels launched derivatives based on either language or program-type such as CNNfn, MSNBC, and MTV Europe. These established channels saw growth opportunity in developing ancillary markets for their brands. The following examples will shed the light on the aims and targets of the main network players.

First established in London, the Middle East Broadcasting Center relocated to the United Arab Emirates in 2003; from there the center launched an aggressive move to attract Arab family viewing. Aiming to maintain Arab values, MBC segmented the audience based on their programming preferences. Consequently, MBC maintained its original programming generalist appeal MBC1, while adding four new services or platforms catering to news (Al-Arabiya), Western movies (MBC 2), kids (MBC 3), and Western series and shows (MBC 4). For example, MBC produced the Arabic versions of *Fear Factor* and *Starting Over*, while MBC 2's lineup rivaled that of TNT and Cinemax. Concurrently, MBC 4 was broadcasting episodes of *60 Minutes*, *The Oprah Winfrey Show*, and seasons of *Friends* and *Frazier*. The children's channel, MBC 3, was originating live call-in shows and dubbing Japanese and American cartoon shows.

Al-Jazeera, which has become a household name worldwide in the wake of the Afghanistan and Iraq invasions, gave the small emirate of Qatar a global presence disproportionate to its size. Recruiting the team of a failed venture by BBC Arabic Television Service, the Qataris in 1996 launched Al-Jazeera as the first Arab 24-hour news channel. Competition from mainly Al-Arabiya led Al-Jazeera to revamp its look and feel, and to move to a new purpose-built facility in June 2005, with an expansion plan based on new channels using the brand image of a hard-hitting and alternative source of news. It also launched a dedicated sports channel, Al-Jazeera sports channels 1 and 2, a C-Span-like service dedicated to covering live events called Al-Jazeera Live and Al-Jazeera Kids. Soon to be launched, Al-Jazeera International will have offices in London, New York, Kuala Lumpur, and an affiliate in Caracas, Venezuela. Al-Jazeera International is poised to become a global news player. Interestingly, Al-Jazeera announced in September 2005 that it would officially change its name from "channel" to "network."

Perhaps the clearest example of the development of a multiplatform "network" is Rotana. As a television channel, Rotana emulated the MTV model. It is however important to note that Rotana is also a leading producer and distributor of records, with more than one hundred artists on its payroll, most of them on exclusive contracts. Rotana's exclusivity requirement is a source of resentment often discussed in the Arab press. From a political-economic perspective, Rotana is leading the way for a simultaneous vertical and horizontal integration in the Arab media market.

After having purchased what is perhaps the largest Arabic-language music-video and performance-video library, which was made possible by the deep pockets of its owner, Saudi royal family member and famed global investor Prince Al Walid Bin Talal, Rotana developed five channels dedicated to various music genres available under the Rotana label, ranging from Arabic song classics by the Egyptian diva Umm Kulthum and her Lebanese colleague Fairuz, to the latest pop tunes by Haifa Wehbe and Nancy Ajram, in addition to Rotana Khaleejiyya specializing in Gulf countries' songs, and Rotana Cinema. These make Rotana a powerful multiplatform media organization and a leading player in Arabic entertainment television.

While Rotana's multiplatform "network" was developed according to a spectrum of media genres and subgenres, the Lebanese Broadcasting

Corporation (LBC) chose a path more congruent with its core Lebanese audience. Taking advantage of the significant Lebanese diaspora in North, Central, and South America; West Africa; Western Europe; and Australia, LBC developed into a platform catering to this scattered and largely prosperous diasporic community. Nagham, one of LBC's channels, was originally designed as a music pay-channel, but is now a dedicated 24-hour, free-to-air reality television channel and airs music videos in the short intervals when LBC has no reality television programs on its schedule. Later with LBC-Al Hayat and LBC international, LBC saw growth opportunity in attracting Arab-speaking audiences beyond its core Lebanese viewership.

DOMINANT ARAB TELEVISION GENRES

Arab satellite television is stunning in its diversity in national origins, styles, and content of programming. In the age of terrestrial channels, programming grids were dominated by national news, some game shows, Egyptian serial dramas, American sitcoms and action series, and the occasional national dramatic production. Today national newscasts have to contend with transnational services like Al-Jazeera and Al-Arabiya, games shows have proliferated, Syrian television dramas compete with Egyptian series, and national productions have somewhat grown. However, three genres have come to dominate Arab satellite television, whether in quantitative terms as per the numbers of hours taken by these genres, or by their impact and their place in public discourse: talk shows, reality television, and music video clips.

Talk Shows

Before the age of the satellite, several national Arab broadcasters had programs that could be broadly classified as talk shows, in that they included a guest and a host, generally in an interview format whereby the former asks questions and the latter answers them. Ziad Noujeim hosted several pioneering talk shows on LBC before moving to the Washington, D.C., area to host Al-Hurra's flagship talk show, *Sa'a Hurra* (*Free Hour*). The tone on these shows was generally low-key, and the ceiling for political speech was clear and rarely reached. There were some exceptions, like the rambunctious *Mashakel wa Houloul* (*Problems and Solutions*) on Tele-Liban, Lebanon's national broadcaster, in the 1980s, where guests engaged in verbal duels and sometimes even screamed at each other. For these kinds of flamboyant discussions to become the fodder of everyday conversation, Arab viewers had to wait for Al-Jazeera's *Al-Ittijah al-Mouakess* (*The*

Opposite Direction) and its boisterous host, Syrian journalist and academic Faysal al-Kassim. Molded after CNN's *Crossfire*, Kassim's show goes far beyond its American inspiration in breaching taboos, passionate tone, and hot-button issues.

The provocative Egyptian media figure Hala Serhan became infamous for hosting shows about incest, masturbation, and other taboo issues on the Egyptian Dream TV, which she left and has recently moved to Rotana. On Al-Arabiya, the Lebanese journalist Gisele Khoury hosts a talk show called *Bil-Arabi, (In Arabic)*, usually a one-on-one interview but sometimes including several in-studio guests. This show is also known for its directness, delivered however in Khoury's trademark insistent-but-gentle questioning style.

On Dubai Television, Daoud al-Sharyan hosts a talk show in which he interviews Arab leaders and public figures, on a station that hosts a variety of talk shows including one dedicated to poetry, which remains popular with Arab viewers, especially those from the Gulf countries. On *Future Television*, the journalist and poet Zahi Wehbe hosts Arab intellectuals and artists. On LBC, Marcel Ghanem leads the successful *Kalam al-Nass (People's Talk)*, where he usually hosts one or several political or journalistic figures, in addition to "specials" on prisoners of war, AIDS as a social problem, and sectarian tensions in Lebanon. This show gained Arab recognition with several Pan-Arab satellite specials where Ghanem hosted high-profile Arab figures. Other talk shows, most of them also inspired by successful U.S. television programs, are very popular with Arab audiences. Among these are MBC's *Kalam Nawaem (Sweet Talk)*, modeled after ABC's *The View*, where four Arab women from Saudi Arabia, Lebanon, Syria, and Tunisia discuss various social and cultural issues with a frankness that some have dubbed revolutionary. Finally, programs like *Lil-Nissa: Fakat (For Women Only)*, dedicated to women's issues ranging from political participation to sexual relations, put the spotlight on women's struggle for their rights in the Arab world.

By moving the parameters for acceptable speech and by staging opposite opinions on issues, talk shows have instituted the culture of argument and pushed out the margins of public discourse. Taking live telephone calls from viewers, in addition to faxes and electronic mail messages, these shows encourage at least the semblance of public participation in debate. Some observers consider talk shows on Arab satellite television to be a combination of the Western journalistic style of aggressive questioning with the Arab tradition of what Jordanian journalist Rami Khoury calls "absolutist" debate. Some of these shows have occasionally degenerated into shouting matches, or hosted guests with extreme, and sometimes racist or anti-Semitic opinions. In spite of these excesses and limits to public participation, these shows have aired some of the diversity of

Arab opinions on dominant political, social, economic, and cultural issues.

Reality Television

A staple in Western media markets, due to low production costs and high
advertising revenues, reality television has also become prevalent on
commercial TV in the Arab world. After several debuts that were more or
less successful and more or less controversial, including the Arabic version of *Who Wants to Be a Millionaire* (on MBC) and the matchmaking show
Al-Hawa Sawa (on ART), the years 2003 and 2004 saw an explosion of programs that attracted record audiences from Morocco to Iraq. Some became a topic of daily conversation for millions of Arabs. More important,
the public discourse surrounding the introduction of reality television to
the region became a space of contention on hot-button issues such as relations between men and women, between Arabs and the West, and
among Arabs themselves, in addition to raising concerns about indigenous cultural creativity and Arab authenticity. In that context, the next
section focuses on the most notable Arab reality television shows: LBC's
Star Academy, Future Television's *Superstar*, and MBC's short-lived *Al-
Rais*. *Star Academy* is the Arabic-language adaptation of an original Dutch
format owned by Endemol, made famous in Lebanon after the French
broadcaster TF1 adapted it for French audiences, in addition to versions
in Quebec, Canada, and Belgium. The first installment, to which this
analysis refers, aired in December 2003 and April 2004. The program's
premise is relatively simple. A group of sixteen people, eight women and
eight men, live together in "The Academy" for four months, where they
take classes, prepare performances, cook, eat, sleep, and interact. Each
week on Friday, the public votes one of two nominees out. *Star Academy*
broke all audience records in the Arab world and became an everyday life
phenomenon. Newspapers devoted columns to attacking or appraising
the program. In Lebanon and Morocco, critical reception was as positive
as popular reception, but *Star Academy* created a crisis in Kuwait and
Saudi Arabia where clerics' virulent attacks were counterbalanced by
enormous popular success. Saudi critics called it "The Other Terrorism"
and a "Whorehouse," while the streets of Jeddah and Riyadh emptied
during Friday broadcasts of the show. In Kuwait, the Islamist block in
Parliament initiated a public questioning of the Minister of Information
for allowing broadcasts, initially voting lack of confidence in the entire
cabinet. Even in countries where it did not trigger public confrontations,
Star Academy entered public discourse.

Future Television's *Superstar* was the Arabic version of *American Idol*. It
staged a singing competition but did not involve secluded shared living

for the contestants. This program registered huge audiences, but did not create as much controversy as *Star Academy*, with the exception of the semifinal of the first installment in 2003. When the Lebanese contestant lost in the semifinal in favor of a Syrian contestant, Lebanese demonstrators stormed the studio and the streets of Beirut in protest to what they saw as a politically motivated decision. With Syria then in control of all the levers of power in Lebanon, the Lebanese had reason to be suspicious. Ultimately, however, Diana Carazon, the Jordanian contestant, won the title of "Superstar of the Arabs." What is remarkable about the *Superstar* finale was that thirty million Arabs watched it and four million voted for contestants. While it would be overly optimistic to believe that reality television is a harbinger of democracy in the Arab world, at a minimum it suggests the democratic and interactive potential of technology serving the public interest (Kraidy 2006).

In contrast to *Star Academy* and *Superstar*'s long, successful lives as Arab-audience favorites, *Al-Rais*, the Arabic version of *Big Brother*, was killed by controversy. Eight days after its launch from a Bahrain studio by the Dubai-based Middle East Broadcasting Center (MBC), *Al-Rais* had to be shut down under the weight of a conflict pitting Bahraini Islamists, politicians, and MBC management. Officially, a scene in which a young man kissed a woman contestant live on the show was the reason for the debacle. However, the airing of the Arabic version of *Big Brother* from Bahrain, one of the conservative Gulf countries, was an opportunity for various groups to air their views and score political points in the public sphere. For Islamists, the program displayed foreign cultural values that were incompatible with Islamic principles. For the growing and powerful business community in the country, shutting down a television program would create bad publicity and scare potential investors away from Bahrain, the self-proclaimed regional leader in Islamic finance and other financial services. For "liberals," it was an opportunity to advocate for a more modern Bahraini Islam. In other words, while ultimately the show went off the air, seeing this episode as a straightforward victory for Islamists misses the complexity of the debate that arose around *Al-Rais* (Kraidy 2006).

Music Video "Clips"

The complexity of the debate over the impact of entertainment television on Arab societies is evident in the debate surrounding music videos, or, as they are known in the region, "video clips." It is difficult to pinpoint a teleological point of origin that would clearly mark the first Arab video clips. Since their inception in the 1960s, national television channels aired national songs with images of national monuments and landscapes.

However, with the advent of satellite television, video clips became an attractive air-filler that capture viewers' attention, are integrated in the commercial synergies between broadcasting and telecommunications, and can be repeated ad infinitum, thus becoming commercially attractive. Music videos are also an excellent promotional tool for albums or songs contributing to the continuous synergies between music, television, and mobile telephony.

The Arab music video industry is concentrated mostly in Beirut and Cairo. This industry saw its main boom during the early 1990s, when the paid music channels of Arab Radio and Television sought program material. Originally, music videos started as clips from concerts or performances. These developed into original scripts with inspiration in Western and Indian music videos. When Rotana bought out ART in 2003, it acquired its catalogue and maintained its practices and tightened its grip on the music industry. Rotana's exclusive music videos cost an average of $40,000 with some even exceeding $100,000, including clips by Lebanese artists Najwa Karam and Majida al-Rumi. Al-Rumi's latest video clip is believed by industry insiders to have cost in excess of $250,000, an enormous sum by regional production standards.

The stars that stoke the flames of controversy are female performers Nancy Ajram from Lebanon and Haifa Wehbi from Egypt. Music videos, along with reality television, have been at the heart of heated debates in the Arab press. Commentators fall broadly in two camps. A first group feels that music videos are essentially an alien import, and the argument most often heard is that if you mute the volume, there was nothing Arab about most music videos. Consequently, music videos are seen as carriers of Western values such as individualism, consumerism, and sexual promiscuity. The second group of commentators regards music videos as a platform for women's liberation from the social and cultural restrictions placed on them in Arab societies. They argue that by displaying women who are not afraid to show their bodies and their feelings, music videos extend the margins of acceptable behavior for Arab women, which in turn has serious social and political implications. Recent developments suggest that the music video industry has expanded its scope to the religious, such as the popular videos of the Muslim singer Sami Yusuf, and the political, such as the "patriotic video clips" that flooded Arab screens after the assassination of Lebanese leader Rafik-al-Hariri in February 2004.

REGIONALIZATION OF THE COMMERCIAL MODEL

Trends in Arab television can be marked by some clear turning points in the history of the industry and broadly described by the policy, technological, and economic forces that shape television in the contemporary Arab world as a commercial for-profit medium. Broad patterns of development have included the regionalization of production and consumption of Arab television, the emergence of specialized, thematic channels that cater to various niche media markets, and the recent emergence of multiplatform "networks," where several channels under one owner combine audience segmentation and large-scale appeal. Dominant television genres, chiefly talk shows in their social and political types, various subgenres in reality television programs, and music video clips have predominated on commercial channels and networks and portend far-reaching social and political controversy in many Arab nations. We reiterate our caveat that dominant trends may change in the near future as the Arab television industry will remain in flux—buffeted by globalization, regional social and political conflict, and the ever-present problem of the Arab-Israeli conflict (including the quest for Palestinian independence) and the U.S. presence in the region, including its occupation of Iraq.

As the transformation of the Arab television industry from a nationally based, state-owned, dirigiste sector toward an increasingly transnational, privately owned, and profit-oriented industry proceeds, there are several issues that will require the attention of scholars interested in Arab media. Among these issues is the question to what extent does the development of Arab television follow a unique historical trajectory? Conversely, to what extent do developments in Arab television follow the media industry globally? This question is important because a comparative approach to Arab media can shed light on issues that would otherwise remain obscure.

On one hand, the increased market liberalization of the Arab media industry reflects a worldwide trend from the Indian subcontinent to South America toward advertising-supported, privately owned, regionally integrated industries. As a result, the Arab screen, like the Indian, French, and Mexican screen, increasingly looks like the American screen, and the implications of such a transformation are too complex to be discussed fully in this chapter. Nonetheless, the Arab television sector is being molded by media globalization, with its standardized industry practices, its transnational program formats, and its increasingly sophisticated visual style. In the Arab world, this is applauded by large swaths of youths and decried by political and religious activists who see cultural globalization as Americanization by another name, which they believe threatens their religious beliefs and social values. Missing from this mediascape are voices advocating for democratic, noncleric, public communication.

On the other hand, the changes experienced by Arab television have a dynamic unique to the Arab region. The volatile mixture of radical Islam, oil wealth, U.S. pressure, and inter-Arab rivalries give a distinct texture to the Arab satellite industry, dominated by Saudi capital and Lebanese and

Egyptian talent, and by intense rivalries. The ferocious rivalry between Al-Jazeera and Al-Arabiya is to a large extent a proxy war between Qatar and Saudi Arabia, and the less public but no less serious competition between MBC and LBC (and to a lesser extent with Future TV) reflects transnational (especially Saudi-Lebanese) business alliances and rivalries within Saudi ruling circles.

Finally, perhaps the most important question is the role that satellite television is playing in the social, cultural, political, and even economic transformation of Arab societies. While programming genres like reality television and video clips often trigger heated controversies of a sociocultural and religious nature, the political and economic roles of satellite television remain to be explored. Many analysts have focused on the presumed democratizing role played by satellite television in the Arab world, enshrining a culture of debate, and giving public platforms for women, dissidents, and intellectuals. However, systematic research on these issues is needed to further examine to what extent the political impact of Arab satellite television advances existing corporate media hegemonic practices or provides opportunities for democratic and independent communication. Finally, there is a need to research the economic impact of Arab television, now that there are several channels specializing in banking and real estate, and to examine the ideological and politico-economic implications of this development.

APPENDIX: MAJOR MEDIA IN THE MIDDLE EAST

All media are private and commercial, unless otherwise noted. English-language media are listed in their English-language titles; Iranian media broadcast and publish in Persian; Israeli, in Hebrew; all others are in Arabic, unless otherwise noted.

SATELLITE TV

Al-Jazeera (influential Pan-Arab satellite broadcaster, financed by the Qatar government)

MBC, Middle East Broadcasting Centre (London-based, owned by the Saudi ARA Group International)

LBC, Lebanese Broadcasting Centre (Saudi Prince Bin Talal owns 49 percent)

STAR (New York–based, owned by News Corp.)

REGIONAL OUTLETS

Bahrain

Bahraini Press
Al-Ayam
Al-Wasat
Bahrain Tribune
Gulf Daily News
Bahraini Television
MBC, Middle East Broadcasting Centre (London-based, owned by ARA Group International

BRTC, Bahrain Radio and Television Corp.

Bahraini Radio
Sawt-al-Ghad (Voice of Tomorrow)
BRTC, Bahrain Radio and Television Corp

Egypt

Egyptian Press
Al-Ahram
Al-Jumhuriyah
Al-Akhbar
Al-Ahali
Al-Wafd
Al-Messa
Middle East Times
Egyptian Television
Egypt Radio Television Union
Dream TV
Egyptian Radio
Nile FM (Western pop)
Nogoum FM (Arabic pop)

Iran

Iranian Press
Aftab-e Yazd
Kayhan
Resalat
Eternaad
Jaam-e Jam
Iran News
Tehran Times
Iran Daily
Iranian Television
IRIB
Iranian Radio
Islamic Radio News
Iranian Student News
Fars News
Iranian Labour News

Iraq

Iraqi Press
Al-Zaman (London-based)
Al-Mashriq
Al-Dustur
Al-Sabah (U.S.–funded)
Iraq Today
Iraqi Television
Al-Sharqiya
Kurdistan Satellite (Kurdistan Democratic Party)
KurdSat (Patriotic Union of Kurdistan)
Al-Hurra (U.S.–funded)
Iraqi Radio
Republic of Iraq (U.S.–funded)
Radio Nahrain (UK–sponsored)
Hot FM
Radio Dijla
Radio Monte Carlo (Paris-based)
Radio Sawa (U.S.–funded)
Radio Free Iraq (U.S.–funded)

Israel

Israeli Press
Yediot Aharonot
Ha-aretz
Jerusalem Post
Ma-ariv
Globes
Israeli Television
Israel Broadcasting Authority (public)
Channel 2 (commercial)
Channel 10 (commercial)
Israeli Radio
Galei Zahal (Israel Defense Forces civilian radio)

Kuwait

Kuwaiti Press
Al-Watan (private, daily)
Al-Qabas (private, daily)
Al-Rai al-Amm (private, daily)
Kuwait Times (English-language)
Arab Times (English-language)
Kuwaiti Television
Kuwaiti TV (state-run, operates three networks and satellite channel)
Al-Rai (first private TV station, via satellite)

Flash TV (private)
Kuwaiti Radio
Radio Kuwait (state-run, programs in English and Arabic)
Marina FM (first private radio station, music-based)
Kuwaiti News Agency
Kuna, Kuwait News Agency (in Arabic and English)

Lebanon

Lebanese Press
An-Nahar (Arabic daily, Allied Media)
Al-Safir (Arabic daily)
Al-Anwar (Arabic daily)
Al-Mustaqbal (Arabic daily)
Al-Diyar (Arabic daily)
Daily Star (English-language)
L'Orient-Le Jour (French-language)
Lebanese Television
Tele-Liban (state-run)
LBC, Lebanese Broadcasting Corporation (commercial, market leader, and pan-regional broadcaster)
Al-Manar TV (pro-Hezbollah)
Future TV (commercial)
Lebanese Radio
Voice of Lebanon (established commercial station)
Radio Liban (state-run)
Radio Delta (commercial)
Radio One (commercial)
Lebanese News Agency
Lebanese National News Agency (state-run)

Libya

Libyan Press
Al-Fajr al-Jadid (MBC)
Al-Shams
Al-Jamahiriyah
Al-Zahf Al-Akhdar
Libyan Television
Great Jamahiriyah TV (state-run, available terrestrially and via satellite)

Libyan Radio
Great Jamahiriyah Radio (state-run)
Voice of Africa (state-run external service, broadcasting in Arabic, English, and French)
Libyan News Agency
Jana, Jamahiriyah News Agency (state-run)

Mauritania

Mauritanian Press
Chaab (in Arabic)
Horizon (in French)
Journal Officiel
Le Calame
L'Eveil-Hebdo
Rajoul Echaree
Nouakchott Info (private daily)
Mauritanian Television
Mauritanian TV (state-run, programs in Arabic, French, and other local languages)
Mauritanian Radio
Radio Mauritania (state-run)
Mauritanian News Agency
AMI, Mauritanian News Agency (state-run)

Morocco

Moroccan Press
Al-Anbaa (government-owned daily)
Le Matin (semi-official daily)
Assabah (private, daily)
Liberation (private, daily)
L'Economiste (business daily)
Le Journal (private, weekly)
Morocco Times (English-language news site)
Moroccan Television
RTM, Radio-Television Marocaine (state-run)
2M (partly state-owned)
Al Maghribiya (satellite channel operated by RTM and 2M, aimed at Moroccans living abroad)

Moroccan Radio
RTM, Radio-Television Marocaine (state-run, regional and national services)
Medi 1 (Tangier-based, privately-owned by Moroccan and French concerns, programs in Arabic and French)
National Radio of the Saharan Arab Democratic Republic (broadcasts in Arabic and Spanish; launched in the 1970s, station supports the Polisario Front, *Western Sahara*)
Moroccan News Agency
MAP, Maghreb Arab Presse (state-run)

Oman

Omani Press
Al-Watan (daily
Oman Daily (Arabic-language daily)
Oman Observer (English-language)
Times of Oman (English-language)
Omani Television
Oman TV (state-run)
Omani Radio
Radio Oman (state-run, operates Arabic and English-language networks)
Omani News Agency
Oman News Agency

Palestine

Palestinian Press
Al-Quds (Jerusalem-based, largest-circulation Palestinian daily, MBC)
Al-Ayyam (Ramallah-based daily)
Al-Hayat Al-Jadidah (Palestinian National Authority daily, MBC)
Palestinian Radio
Voice of Palestine (official)
Palestinian Television
Palestine TV (official)
Palestine Satellite Channel (official, Gaza-based)
Private TV (stations include Al-Quds Educational TV, Al-Mahd TV, Al-Majd TV, Al-Nawras TV, Al-Sharq TV [MBC], Amwaj TV, Bayt Lahm TV, Shepherds TV, and Watan TV)

Palestinian News Agency
Wafa , Palestine News Agency (official, in Arabic, English, French, and Hebrew)

Qatar

Qatari Press
Al-Watan (daily)
Gulf Times (English-language)
The Peninsula (English-language)
Qatari Television
Al-Jazeera (influential Pan-Arab satellite broadcaster, financed by the Qatar government)
Qatar TV (state-run, operates main Arabic service, Koran channel, English channel, satellite channel)
Qatari Radio
QBS, Qatar Broadcasting Service (state-run)

Saudi Arabia

Saudi Press
Al-Madina
Al-Riyadh
Al-Watan
Al-Yaum
Al-Bilad
Al-Jazirah
Okaz
Arab News/Saudi Gazette
Saudi Television
Saudi TV-Channel 1
Saudi TV-Channel 2
Al-Ekhbariya
Saudi Radio
 MBC FM
Al Ekhbariya

Syria

Syrian Press
Al-Baath
Al-Thawra

Teshreen
Al-Maukef Al-Riadi (sports)
Syria Times
Syrian Television
Syria TV
Syrian Radio
Syria Radio

Turkey

Turkish Press
Aksam
Hurriyet
Teshreen
Milliyet
Sabah
Turkiye
Zaman
Turkish Daily News
Turkish Television
Kanal D
NTV MSNBC
STV
TRT (state-run)
Turkish Radio
TRT Radio (state-run)
Show Radyo (commercial)
Capital Radio (commercial, pop)
Rady Foreks (news)

United Arab Emirates

Emirate Press
Akhbar Al-Arab
Al-Bayan
Al-Ittihad
Al-Khaleej
Emarat Al Youm
Emirates Today
Gulf News

Khaleej Times
Emirates Evening Post
Emirate Television
Abu-Dhabi TV
Dubai TV
Sama Dubai
Sharjah TV
Al-Arabiya
Emirate Radio
Abu Dhabi AM
Al Khaleejiah
Abu Dhabi Emarat FM
Abu Dhabi Sound of Music
Dubai Eye
Abu Dhabi Quran Kareem'
Sout Al Asala
Al-Arabiya
Channel 4 FM
Dubai 92
Emirates 2 FM
City FM (Hindi)
Radio 4 FM (Hindi)
Hum (Hindi)
Asianet Radio (Malayalam)
Hit 96.7 FM (Malayalam)

Yemen

Yemeni Press
Al-Ayyam
Al-Guhuryah
Al-Thawra
Yemen Times (weekly)
Yemen Observer (weekly)
Yemeni Television
Republic of Yemen TV
Yemeni Radio
Aden Radio
Sana'a Radio
Republic of Yemen Radio

References

Amin, H. Y., and Boyd, D. A. (1994). "The development of direct broadcast television to and within the Middle East." *Journal of South Asia and Middle Eastern Studies* 18(2), pp. 37–50.

ARABSAT. (1997) "Second-generation satellites." Riyadh: ARABSAT.

"ARABSAT's general manager: We have pointed CFI's attention since 1993 on their violation of our contract" (1997, July 27). *Asharq Al-Awsat* (The Middle East) 16, p. 1.

Artz, L. (2003). "Globalization, media hegemony, and social class." In L. Artz and Y. Kamalipour (eds.), *The globalization of corporate media*, pp. 3–31. Albany: State University of New York.

Ayish, M. I. (1997). "Arab television goes commercial: A case study of the Middle East Broadcasting Center." *Gazette* 59(6), pp. 473–494.

Barkey, M. (1996, January). "Satellite TV: On the eve of revolution." *Arab Ad*, pp. 12–14.

Boulos, J. C. (1996). *La télé: Quelle histoire (Television: What a story)*. Beyrouth: Fiches du Monde Arabe.

Boyd, D. A. (1991). "Lebanese broadcasting: Unofficial electronic media during a prolonged civil war." *Journal of Broadcasting and Electronic Media* 35(3), pp. 269–287.

—— (1993). "A new 'line in the sand' for the media." *Media Studies Journal* 7(4), pp. 133–140.

—— (1999). *Broadcasting in the Arab world: A survey of the electronic media in the Middle East*. Ames: Iowa State University.

Fakhreddine, J. (2000). "Pan-Arab satellite television: Now the survival part." *Transnational Broadcasting Studies* 5. At www.tbsjournal.org (accessed October 1, 2005).

Gher, L. A., and Amin, H. Y., eds. (2000). *Civic discourse and digital age communications in the Middle East*. Stamford, Conn.: Ablex.

Kazan, N. (1996, November). "A winner in the booming satellite industry." *Arab Ad*, pp. 6–12.

Kraidy, M. M. (1998a). "Satellite broadcasting from Lebanon: Prospects and perils." *Transnational Broadcasting Studies* 1. At www.tbsjournal.org (accessed October 1, 2005).

—— (1998b). "Broadcasting regulation and civil society in post-war Lebanon." *Journal of Broadcasting and Electronic Media* 42(3), pp. 387–400.

—— (1999a). "The local, the global and the hybrid: A native ethnography of glocalization." *Critical Studies in Media Communication* 16(4), pp. 456–477.

—— (1999b). "State control of television news in 1990s Lebanon." *Journalism and Mass Communication Quarterly* 76(3), pp. 485–498.

—— (2000a). "Transnational satellite television and asymmetrical interdependence in the Arab world: A research note." *Transnational Broadcasting Studies* 5. At www.tbsjournal.org (accessed October 1, 2005).

—— (2000b). "Television and civic discourse in postwar Lebanon." In L. A. Gher and H. Y. Amin (eds.), *Civic discourse and digital age communications in the Middle East*, pp. 3–18. Stamford, Conn.: Ablex.

—— (2001). "National television between localization and globalization." In Y. Kamalipour and K. Rampal (eds.), *Media, sex, violence, and drugs in the global village*, pp. 261. Lanham, Md.: Rowman and Littlefield.

—— (2002). "Arab television between regionalization and globalization." *Global Media Journal* 1(1). At www.globalmediajournal.com (accessed October 1, 2005).

—— (2005). *Hybridity, or the cultural logic of globalization*. Philadelphia: Temple University Press.

—— (2006). "Hypermedia and governance in Saudi Arabia." In Sandra Braman and Thomas Malaby (eds.), *Command lines: Governance in cyberspace*. New Brunswick, N.J.: Rutgers University.

Overview (1997). Riyadh: ARABSAT.

Russell, P. (1994, November). "Roman roads lead to new orbits." *TV World*, pp. 28–29.

Saadé, J. (1997, November 11). "LBCI faces legal quiz over Tamraz talk show." *Daily Star*. At www.dailystar.com.lb/11-11-97/art2.htm (accessed October 1, 2005).

Sabeh (1997, January 22). "No censorship on media freedom and satellite issue will enjoy 'home' treatment." *An-Nahar*, p. 4.

"Satellite generations" (2002, September 2002). ARABSAT. At www.arabsat.com/satgen/index.asp (accessed October 14, 2005).

"Satellite programs and the telephone calls they generate are the reason" (1997, January 23). *An-Nahar*, p. 6.

"Saudis clamp down on satellite viewing" (1996). *Arab Ad* 6, p. 67.

Schleifer, S. A. (1998). "Media explosion in the Arab world: The Pan-Arab satellite broadcasters." *Transnational Broadcasting Studies* 1. At www.tbsjournal.org (accessed October 1, 2005).

—— (2000). "Does satellite TV pay in the Arab world footprint? Exploring the economic feasibility of specialized and general channels." *Transnational Broadcasting Studies* 5. At www.tbsjournal.org (accessed October 1, 2005).

Tawil, F. (1997). "Saudi media scene evolution." *Arab Ad* 7, pp. 8–10.

Temko, N. (1984, August 14). "Why ordinary Arabs faithfully turn to the voice of the 'enemy.'" *Christian Science Monitor*, p. 1.

5

Latin America:
Media Conglomerates

José-Carlos Lozano

During the 1970s most Latin American communication scholars de-
nounced the hegemony of American media and media flows in the
region. Today, an increasing number of scholars in this region have em-
braced new theoretical concepts like "cultural proximity," "cultural discount," and "cultural linguistic markets" that promote more optimistic
views about the development of the Latin American audiovisual space.

During the 1970s and early 1980s, scholars like Beltrán (1978), Beltrán
and Fox (1980), García Calderón (1987), Dorfman (1980), Mattelart (1974),
Santa Cruz and Erazo (1981), Pasquali (1972) analyzed and discussed the
Latin American media dependency on U.S. media, as well as the ideological domination stemming from their messages and even from the local
content modeled after foreign messages. Some of the concluding remarks
in the influential book *Dominated communication: The United States in Latin
American media*, by Luis Beltrán and Elizabeth Fox (1980), are examples of
the positions adopted by most Latin American theorists at the time:

1. The Latin American mass media system is so dependent on U.S. economic, political, and communication institutions that it is possible to
   refer to it as a case of domination.
2. The vast majority of the main mass media in the region, especially
   the electronic media, are directly or indirectly influenced by large
   American interests.
3. In the news flows in Latin America, U.S. content exceeds by far local
   content. With respect to movies, foreign films represent more than

half of the total. The proportion of U.S. TV programs is on average one-third.

4. U.S. superiority is so strong it represents a danger for the autonomy of Latin American communication, particularly if qualitative factors of impact are taken into account. (p. 152)

During the 1980s and the 1990s, however, several scholars in different parts of the world found empirical evidence for the development of local and regional markets and for the preference of audiences for their local and regional productions over American ones. Antola and Rogers, in 1984, found that the 52 percent of U.S. TV imports in Latin American media documented by Nordenstreng and Varis in their 1973 study, had decreased to only 29 percent ten years after in their own study of six countries (Mexico, Brazil, Venezuela, Peru, Chile, and Argentina). They argued that U.S. imports had decreased in those countries and that local productions were more popular than U.S. productions, according to the ratings. They also explained that the initial dependency of local television systems on U.S. audiovisual conglomerates, instead of hindering their internal and regional development, had allowed their consolidation and growth to the point they were able to cut their initial ties and overcome economic and technological dependency. In most cases, American productions like *Dallas* were easily beaten in the ratings battle by local or regional productions. In a follow-up of his original 1973 study, however, Varis (1984) found that in many Latin American countries the percentage of foreign imports was still 77 percent ten years later.

In 1989, an article by Hoskins, Mirus, and Rozeboom would provide more evidence to qualify the original assertions of cultural imperialists. According to the authors, one of the main reasons for the popularity of U.S. exports in Latin America (as in the rest of the world) was their low cost due to their revenues in their own domestic market, the largest and most prosperous in the world. If the exportation cost to the rest of the world is in general too low (on average one hundred times lower than its original cost), it is even cheaper for non-Anglo-Saxon countries due to a factor that may seem ironic: the "cultural discount" phenomenon. U.S. exporters need to lower the cost of their products in markets with low linguistic and cultural affinity because their products are less attractive. Thus, if in Canada each half hour of U.S. imported programs in the mid-1980s had a cost of from $15,000 to $20,000, in Mexico the same half hour had a cost of only around $1,400 to $2,000 (p. 56). The size of the audience, the number of buyers in each country, and the per capita product of each nation were also important when explaining the cost, but after controlling statistically for these variables, cultural proximity was able to explain by itself the final cost of imports, showing that importing U.S. audiovisual products in cultures different from the American culture resulted in a discount that impacted the cost.

Around the same date, Straubhaar et al. (1994) used the phrase *cultural proximity* to explain why, all other things being equal, audiences would tend to prefer programming that is closest or most proximate to their own culture, their own national productions if they could be supported by the local economy or regional programming over content from more distant countries or cultures. Thus, "the United States continues to have an advantage primarily in genres that even large Third World countries cannot afford to produce, such as feature films, cartoons, and action-adventure series" (p. 81). In his 1994 article, Straubhaar also advanced the concept of "asymmetrical interdependence" to use instead of "dependence," a concept cultural imperialists used to analyze the relations between developed and developing countries.

In a longitudinal content analysis about the origin of TV programs transmitted in 1962, 1972, 1982, and 1991 in several Asian, Latin American, North American, and Caribbean countries, Straubhaar et al. (1994) found limited support for the concept of cultural proximity. Local production increased in most countries, doing very well in prime time, but in the smallest developing countries, U.S. imports were still predominant over local and regional content. The findings also partially supported the assertion about regional productions being more popular than more culturally distant messages (like the American ones), particularly in Latin America, where small countries like the Dominican Republic imported more programs from Latin American countries such as Mexico and Brazil than from the United States (p. 143). In a later work, Straubhaar et al. (2003) updated their study up to 2001, this time including the countries of Mexico, Colombia, and Venezuela, as well as Canada. Their findings in this study were more conclusive, clearly supporting the concept of cultural proximity. National productions had increased overall in the period of study and had increased their presence in prime time. The national production capacity and the demand for national programming also increased. They conclude the presence of national programming in prime time is a clear indication of the tendency toward cultural proximity (p. 23). Also, they point out the utility of the asymmetrical interdependence theoretical framework when identifying the wide spectrum of possibilities and developments related to national and regional production in different developing countries: "The more affluent Asian countries, as well as the poorer but bigger Brazil, seem able to produce much more than the smaller Latin American countries" (p. 24).

The objective of this chapter is to summarize the empirical evidence to date about the supply and consumption of local, national, and foreign TV and film content in different Latin American countries and to discuss this in relation to the current debate between cultural proximity advocates and political economists. First, I discuss recent developments in the consolidation and expansion of Latin American media conglomerates and their links and alliances with other regional and transnational groups. Second, I look at current flows of TV content within Latin American countries, tracking the volume of regional exports and imports. Finally, I discuss the ratings of these imports in different countries of the region, comparing them with the ratings of local productions.

PRESENT PERFORMANCE OF THE LATIN AMERICAN CULTURAL LINGUISTIC MARKET

How is the Latin American linguistic market doing with respect to the structure of regional media and media flows between the countries of the region? Are U.S. imports more predominant than regional imports? Are regional imports more likely to be found in some particular media or genre?

In relation to the structure of the Latin American media, there is evidence of an important development of regional conglomerates with links and strategic alliances between them. There are at least four large Latin American media conglomerates: Grupo Clarín in Argentina, Televisa in Mexico, Globo in Brazil, and Grupo Cisneros in Venezuela. They are not the only groups, but they are the largest and the ones with tighter links between them and with other smaller regional or local groups.

Grupo Clarín, for example, has links with media enterprises in Paraguay, Guatemala, and Puerto Rico, in alliance with the Venezuelan Cisneros Group in the last two countries. Televisa, on the other hand, owns or has alliances with TV stations in Brazil, Chile, Ecuador, Guatemala, Paraguay, Peru, and the United States, among other countries. Televisa owns 15 percent of the shares of Univisión and supplies 40 percent of its programming, while the Cisneros Group owns 19 percent of the shares and supplies 11 percent of its programming. Joe Perenchio owns the other 66 percent. The Cisneros Group has links or owns media in Argentina, Brazil, Guatemala, the United States, and Puerto Rico (Arroyo, López, and Vega 2003) and boasts ownership of six media networks in the hemisphere (Colitt 1998). Also, this Venezuelan group has bought shares in the last few years in Latin American, Spanish, and Portuguese media, trying to become the major shareholder of local media groups:

> "On your own it's going to take you longer and cost you more money," says Carlos Cisneros. An appropriate partner, he says, adds efficiency and speed to the operation. "Speed is becoming an incredibly important part of anybody's strategy in Latin America, which is moving faster than any other market in the world. (Colitt 1998)

According to Colitt, in 1998 the Cisneros Group acquired Imagen Satelital, Argentina's largest cable programmer, and gave management options to buy a 20 percent stake. Also, it signed in 2001 an agreement with Admira (owned by Telefónica España) to coproduce *telenovelas* for the Latin American and Hispanic markets in the United States (De Pablos 2003).

Televisa is partner of the Prensa Española Company, a part of Grupo Europroducciones, to coproduce *telenovelas* for Spain (Hopewell 2001, July 30–August 5). After a decline in the interest of Spanish audiences for Latin American *telenovelas*, the new strategy of bringing scripts produced by Televisa in Mexico and rewritten for the Spanish market seems to be working.

In June 2004, Globo, the Brazilian giant audiovisual conglomerate, sold 49 percent of its shares of Net, its cable TV subsidiary, to the Mexican telecommunications conglomerate Telmex (Duarte 2005, p. 336), although Globo may be the Latin American conglomerate with fewer regional ties (Rebouças 2005). According to Rebouças, Globo has made very little effort in strategic terms to extend its influence in Latin America: "Except for exporting *telenovelas* to an extremely competitive market, the transnationalization of Globo has not happened" (p. 157). Instead of making partnership with other regional groups or investing in other Latin American countries, Globo has opted for commercializing one paid-TV channel, "TV Globo Internacional," in countries like Portugal, several Latin American countries, and the United States (Brittos 2005a, pp. 143–145).

These large Latin American media conglomerates, despite their economic power and their production capacity—or maybe because of this—have links and clear alliances with the giant media multinationals (characterized as transnationals by Lee Artz in his contribution to this book). Grupo Clarín is partner in Argentina of DIRECTV Latin America, owned by Hughes Electronics (Sutter 2001). Televisa and Globo are partners of SKY Latin America, along with News Corporation and Liberty Media. Televisa also has commercial ties with Entretenimiento Plural, a subsidiary of the large Spanish group PRISA, to produce films, movies for TV, and miniseries (De Pablos 2003). The U.S. Gaylord Cable Networks is the partner of local Argentinean groups in the music channels MusicCountry Latin America and Tango, as well as the Mexican channel Video Rola in Guadalajara (Cobo 2001, February 17). Peruvian cable system Cable Magico has links with Telefonica (Spain) (Sutter 2001, March 26–April 1). Venezuelan cable company MSO Super Cable is partially owned by the U.S. group MSO Adelphia Cable Communication, direct owner of 20 percent of the shares, and another 20 percent of the shares through its Ecuadorian subsidiary Eljuri, considered a local partner by the Andian pact despite its dependence on the U.S. company (Duarte 1999). Chase Manhattan, Capital Cities/ABC, The Hearst Corporation, and Falcon

International Communications were partners in the late 1990s of the Brazilian cable television company TVA, a subsidiary of Grupo Abril (Brittos 2005b, p. 74). In 2001, Globo signed an agreement with Telemundo, an AT&T and Sony enterprise at the time (but a recent NBC/GE acquisition), to produce fifteen thousand hours of programming in a five-year term, starting with some *telenovelas* that were not that successful (Rebouças 2005). The Venezuelan Cisneros Group joined forces with Hicks, Muse, Tate and Furst, a U.S. company, to launch Claxson Interactive Group Inc., an integrated provider of entertainment content for Spanish- and Portuguese-language markets.

According to Cisneros Web page,

> Claxson television channels reach over 10 million households and 46.5 million viewers on cable and direct-to-home platforms throughout Ibero-America, and include some of the most popular pay channels in the Southern Cone. The company operates Playboy TV Latin America and Iberia, a joint venture with Playboy Enterprises. In addition, Claxson owns regional broadcast television and Internet operations, and the largest radio broadcasting company in Chile in terms of revenue, audience share and number of stations. The company's post-production facilities dub and package proprietary and international television content for distribution across Ibero-America and the world. (Cisneros Group of Companies)

In 1995 the Cisneros Group and GM Hughes Electronics became partners in DIRECTV Latin America, the pioneer in direct-to-home satellite television to Latin America and the Caribbean. Now a News Corporation company, DIRECTV Latin America reaches twenty-seven countries including Argentina, Brazil, Chile, Colombia, Costa Rica, Ecuador, El Salvador, Guatemala, Honduras, Nicaragua, Panama, Puerto Rico, Trinidad and Tobago, Uruguay, Venezuela, and several Caribbean island nations (DIRECTV n.d.).

Sometimes, these multinational conglomerates are direct owners of important media. This is the case of the Canadian network CTG, owner of the music channel MuchMusic in Argentina and of the previously mentioned Gaylord Cable Networks, which is the exclusive owner of the channel MusicCountry in Brazil (Cobo 2001, February 17). The Spanish Arbol Group owns the Argentinian company Promofilm, distributor of reality shows in Colombia and Venezuela like *Protagonistas de Novela* and the variety show *Sala de Parejas* for Colombia, Venezuela, and the United States (De Pablos 2003, January 20–26). In 2000, the French MultiThematiques company acquired the Brazilian Eurochannel cable channel from the Latin American group Abril. The channel transmits European movies, sitcoms, and documentaries 24 hours per day (James 2000, November 20–26). In fact, not only American and European media conglomerates, but also cities, like Miami, have an extraordinary influence in Latin American TV programming, as Sinclair (2003) explains. Miami is the headquarters for channels like MTV Latino and of the Hispanic networks Telemundo (owned by NBC) and Univisión (owned by Perenchio, Televisa, and the Cisneros Group). The latter has facilities in Miami for the production of content geared to the region (p. 224). Its rival RCTV has a distribution company in the United States called Coral Pictures. This particular situation makes the analysis of the Latin American regional markets more complicated, due to the existence of a U.S. city used as a platform for the production and distribution of content for the region.

To summarize, while on the one hand large Latin American media conglomerates have developed and consolidated (showing that U.S. dominance is not absolute), on the other hand the American and multinational media giants still provide leadership and expertise for media practices in the region, especially through foreign direct investment, joint ventures, and other transnational activities (see Artz essay, this text).

LATIN AMERICAN TV FLOWS

Several findings suggest TV flows originating in Latin American countries and distributed to other countries in the region have increased in the last few years, in tune with the hypothesis of cultural proximity. According to Luis Villanueva, president of Venevision Intl., during the year 2000 more than sixty-five thousand hours of *telenovela* programming was purchased in Latin America alone (Sutter 2001, January 15–21). On the other hand, Sutter asserts that during the same year Televisa sold ninety thousand hours of different programs to the rest of the world, particularly Latin America. To make its *telenovelas* more attractive, Televisa uses neutral Spanish and includes Colombian and Venezuelan actors. The same is true in the case of Venevision, which uses Venezuelan and Mexican actors in its Miami productions. In 2002, Brazilian Globo, another of the big exporters, started the production of its first *telenovela* geared specifically to the Hispanic audience in the United States: *Vale Todo (Everything Goes)*. Based on a Brazilian *telenovela*, the story was adapted and includes Mexican characters living in Rio de Janeiro, using neutral Spanish and limiting the sensual content characteristic of the original version ("Profile: Brazilian network" 2002). According to Davis (2003), in 1995 Ecuador imported almost 40 percent of its prime-time TV programming from Venezuela, Brazil, and Mexico, a little more than the percentage of imports from the United States (p. 117). In September 2003, eleven Televisa productions, mainly *telenovelas*, were shown on Venezuelan television ("Gotita" 2003). In Paraguay, a 1995 study revealed that 24 percent of the programs on channels 9 and 13 of Asuncion were imported from Latin American countries and only 24 percent came from the United States (Brunetti 1996, pp. 85–86). The cases of Brazil, Mexico, and to a lesser extent Argentina and

Venezuela also validate the assertions by cultural proximity advocates that audiences select local productions over regional or American productions when they have the chance. This is true also for countries with a lower volume of productions, like Chile, where the network Television Nacional de Chile (TVN) got a higher rating than its rivals through local *telenovelas* (Sutter 2001, January 15–21). In a review of studies about imports on Mexican TV from 1980 through 2003, Lozano (2003) found the percentage of American programs during those twenty-three years on the Mexican open-TV channels fluctuated between 28 percent and 49 percent of the total from 6 a.m. to 12 a.m., and from 31 to 49 percent in prime time, the lower percentages belonging to the more recent years (tables 5.1 and 5.2). Straubhaar et al. (2003) found that in 2001, local productions in Brazil, Chile, Colombia, and Mexico represented between 66 percent and 83 percent of prime time (table 5.3). TV programs originating in the United States, on the other hand, occupied only 8 percent of total prime time in Brazil, 14 percent in Chile, 13 percent in Colombia, and 27 percent in Mexico (table 5.4), significantly lower percentages than predicted by cultural imperialists.

However, these figures are less optimistic if we look at the percentages of imports by genre. It is possible to see a clear predominance of U.S. imports in the case of fiction. In Mexico, for example, U.S. content occupied from 45 to 72 percent of total fiction time (table 5.5). U.S. imports predominate also in Latin American paid-television. According to IBOPE, the combined ratings of Argentina, Brazil, Chile, Colombia, Mexico, and Peru show the ten preferred channels on paid-TV were U.S. channels (Zona Latina 2006). Although subscription figures are low in Latin America for paid-TV (from 15 to 30 percent in most countries, with the exception of Argentina), the tendencies show that in this medium U.S. contents are more attractive.

THE PREDOMINANCE OF U.S. MOVIES IN LATIN AMERICA

While regional imports like *telenovelas* receive higher ratings, there is an American genre that is extremely popular with Latin American audiences: fiction. Most open-TV stations transmit a great number of U.S. movies, and some drama series or sitcoms. What is the reason for this? Why is it that cultural proximity does not seem to work in this particular case? If we compare the ratings of *telenovelas* and of U.S. films, we see that the cultural proximity hypothesis seems to work fine. However, U.S. films occupied a significant proportion of total time in many of the TV stations. One of the main reasons for this is the low cost of this kind of import in a region that imposes a discount for differences in culture and language. In addition, Latin American countries are not big producers of films, so U.S. movies do not compete with local or regional films. *Telenovelas* are scheduled in the most popular times of the day and on the most popular channels, and U.S. movies are programmed on channels or in time slots aimed at audiences not interested in the prime Latin American genre, or they are used to fill in times open to all kinds of audiences. TV Globo, for example, produces locally up to 78 percent of its total programming time and 98 percent of its prime time, but transmits around twelve U.S. movies per week (Sutter, 2001, May 21–27). Its main competitor, SBT, schedules U.S. movies in prime time, frequently receiving higher ratings than Globo. In fact, SBT has an exclusive agreement with Disney Movies and Warner Bros., signed in 2000 and good for five years (Sutter 2001). In Mexico, Televisa transmits only its own productions on its flagship channel, channel 2, but includes many U.S. movies and series on its channel 5 and on its other two national channels. Its rival, TV Azteca, also transmits U.S. movies and series on its national channel 7, and up to the year 2001 had an exclusive agreement with Disney.

Although the presence of American content is higher on paid-TV channels, the coverage of these systems in Latin America is much weaker. Of approximately eighty-three million households in Latin America with open-TV, less than 10 percent subscribed to any form of paid-TV in 1996 (Covington 1996, May 8). These figures have increased significantly in the last few years, but they are still far from reaching the coverage of open-TV.

The Latin American groups have tried recently to reinforce regional production of films imitating some of the tactics of European companies. Since movies made in one country do not work well in another, they have started to make coproductions. One of the most ambitious cases is that of the Argentinean company Patagonik (owned by Grupo Clarín, Buena Vista International, Telefonica Media, and Bossi) with the Spanish company Tornasol, to coproduce twelve movies for TV that are based on adaptations of Latin American literary works (Hopewell 2001).

LOCAL AND REGIONAL PREFERENCES
OF LATIN AMERICAN AUDIENCES

The scheduling of local and regional programs in prime time on most Latin American TV stations suggests audiences prefer them to U.S. imports. However, this is an assertion that needs to be verified by looking at the ratings. Several studies provide supporting evidence that Latin American audiences prefer local or regional productions, in line with the findings of many culturalist studies in the rest of the world (cf. Biltereyst 1992; Caron and Bélanger 1993; De la Garde 1993). In Mexico, several studies from the 1980s to date have concluded that Mexican audiences strongly prefer local over foreign content (De la Garza 1996; De la Peña 1998; Díaz 1995; Figueroa 1996; García 1997; Lozano 1995/1996, 1997, 2003; Sánchez Ruiz 1994/1995). The same studies, however, have found an exception: male upper-class youngsters, who tend to like U.S. imports a lot, while still consuming national programs. In the global rating of cities like Mexico City and Monterrey, for example, there were few foreign programs on the list of preferences. Among youngsters of Monterrey, Irapuato, and Mexico City, however, U.S. programs like *The Simpsons*, *Fresh Prince of Bel Air*, and *Beverly Hills 90210* were frequently mentioned as the most popular, particularly among upper-class youngsters. We can conclude, according to these studies, that a large number of youngsters watch U.S. imports, although the specific percentage oscillated from 24 percent of lower socioeconomic status (SES) in Irapuato up to 83 percent of upper SES youngsters in Mexico City. Most studies, however, found that lower and middle SES youngsters still liked local productions more than foreign ones. This suggests the existence of cultural processes and practices associated with the SES that create obvious differences in the consumption of TV messages.

Ratings for Ecuador in 1995 show a significant preference for local and regional programs (see Davis 2003). Sixteen of the twenty programs with the highest popularity among audiences in Quito and Guayaquil were from Latin America (including Ecuador itself). Some U.S. programs made the top-ten list in each city, but none were ranked first (p. 121). The same was true in the case of Argentina, where according to IBOPE, the five programs with the highest ratings in October 2003 in each of the five main open-TV channels in metropolitan Buenos Aires, in prime time, were locally produced ("Top 5" 2003).

Venezuela was an important contrasting case, showing that not all Latin American countries adhere to the cultural proximity concept. AGB ratings for the week of July 21–27, 2003, show that half the programs listed in the ten programs with the highest ratings in open-air TV (Channels RCTV and Venevision) originated in the United States ("Ranking" 2003).

THE CONCEPT OF ASYMMETRICAL INTERDEPENDENCE REVISITED

No doubt, the cultural proximity principle works by and large in Latin America: the current production and consumption patterns are far from showing a predominance of U.S. imports. However, there are some points to be made:

1. Latin American TV systems may be owned by local capitalist enterprises, but historically they developed following the guidelines of U.S. consultants and technicians. They still follow the commercial television model of the United States and their main goal remains profit. Visions of the world transmitted in local content may not be strikingly different from their U.S. counterparts, because private broadcasting

across Latin American belongs to local and regional capitalist classes, which share interests and values with the U.S. capitalist media.

2. Regional media groups' partners, to an increasing extent, are U.S. or European media conglomerates. These partners very frequently impose structures and processes compatible with their own structures and processes (Biltereyst and Meers 2000, p. 396).

3. Many small Latin American countries still show high percentages of U.S. imports. U.S. imports in Ecuador, for example, account for 38 percent of prime time on its national channels (Davis 2003). Larger countries like Mexico, which are big producers of local content, show a tendency predicted by the cultural proximity concept, going from up to 42 percent in U.S. imports in the 1980s and early 1990s to the current 27 percent in prime time (Lozano 2000, 2004).

4. In some genres (movies, series, sitcoms, and cartoons) U.S. dominance is still significant, despite their lack of cultural proximity. The reasons for this are mainly economic (very high costs make these products impossible to be replicated by local media on a systematic basis). However, the fact is large Latin American audiences are being exposed to high volumes of these types of content without consistent local or regional alternatives.

These points suggest the need to adopt a more critical position when considering the development of the Latin American geolinguistic audiovisual market and to give careful consideration to the position of European and Latin American political economists. I would not advocate a return to the more reductive representations of the 1970s cultural imperial theorists. But if in the field of cultural studies current debates question the excessive optimism of scholars stressing the negotiating capacity of audiences (cf. Curran 1990; Morley 1993), it would be welcomed to have the same debate in a field where celebratory visions have become the new fashion. In fact, Biltereyst and Meers (2000) have called these celebratory positions about cultural proximity and local or regional TV preferences "revisionists," adopting the same term used by Curran for overoptimistic culturalists. Both scholars provide convincing arguments and data about the specific case of Latin American *telenovelas* exported to Europe. They argue that the apparent success of these programs (called by some scholars "reversed cultural imperialism") was short-lived and limited, and they argue that currently the number of *telenovelas* has decreased due to growing competition with local productions and the decision of program managers to go back to the more reliable and time-tested U.S. imports. This is not the case, however, for the Latin American regional flows, which show vitality and relevance as discussed above. What we need for the Latin American audiovisual space, consequently, is a more critical vision able to take into account both what the cultural proximity approach has documented about regional flows and the growth of regional groups, and what the political economists document in relation to the persistence of transnational economic interests and relevant percentages of U.S. imports. The debate must be open and permanent between both approaches and needs to take into account reliable and valid empirical research work able to facilitate more knowledge in this field.

APPENDIX: TABLES 5.1 THROUGH 5.5

Note: D.F. in tables is the Federal District, the federal capitol of Mexico (Mexico City).

Table 5.1. Percentage of Foreign Programming in Mexico by Type of System and City

Study	Year	% of Foreign Contents [Content] OpenTV	Paid TV	Cities Included in the Study
Sánchez Ruiz (1992)	1981	30		
Sánchez Ruiz (1996)	1983	34[1] (29)[2]		D.F. & Guadalajara
Sánchez Ruiz (1996)	1984	31(24)		D.F. & Guadalajara
Sánchez Ruiz (1996)	1990	31(23)		D.F. & Guadalajara
Crovi (1995a)	1994	35		D.F.
Figueroa (1996)	1994	49	82	D.F.
Blanco (1996)	1994	48	74	Irapuato
Sánchez Ruiz (1996)	1995	47 (37)		D.F., Guadalajara, Leon & Uruapan
Crovi y Vilar (1995)	1995	42		D.F.
Orozco y Viveros (1996)	1995	48		D.F.
Díaz (1995)	1995	28 (19)	78 (66)	Monterrey
Sánchez Ruiz (1995)	1995	44 (33)		Guadalajara
Lozano (1995/96)		1995	59%	Percentage of channels in Cablevisión, DF originated in USA
			95%	Number of channels in Multivisión, D.F. originated in USA
			60%	Number of channels in Monterrey originated in USA
Lozano y Huerta (2001)	1999	46, 37, 38, 37 (40, 32, 32, 32)		Four weeks of 1999 of four national channels, one for each trimester
Lozano & Martinez (2004)	2003	35.6 (27.4)		12 weeks of 2003 of four national channels, one for each month

[1] Percentage of foreign programming
[2] Percentage of U.S. programming

Table 5.2.   Percentage of Foreign Programming in Mexico by Type of System and City: Prime Time

Study	Year	% of Foreign Contents [Content] OpenTV	[Content] Paid TV	Cities Included in the Study
Sánchez Ruiz (1996)	1981	48		D.F. & Guadalajara
Sánchez Ruiz (1996)	1983	46[1] (44)[2]		D.F. & Guadalajara
Sánchez Ruiz (1996)	1984	46 (40)		D.F. & Guadalajara
Sánchez Ruiz (1996)	1990	46 (34)		D.F. & Guadalajara
Blanco (1996)	1994	55	71	Irapuato
Sánchez Ruiz (1996)	1995	52 (42)		D.F., Guadalajara, León & Uruapan
Lozano y García (1995)	1995	50 (42)		Monterrey
Sánchez Ruiz (1995)	1995	50 (38)		Guadalajara
Lozano & Huerta (2001)	1999	(31)		Four weeks of 1999 of four national channels, one for each trimester
Lozano & Martinez (2004)	2003		31(27)	Average of 12 weeks of 2003 of four national channels (one for each month)

[1] Percentage of foreign programming
[2] Percentage of U.S. programming

Table 5.3. Percentage of Prime Time and Global Time Per Day Occupied by Programs Produced Locally in Several Latin American Countries

	1962		1972		1982		1991		2001	
	Prime time	Global	Prime time	Global	Prime time	Global	Prime time	Global	Prime time	Global
Brazil	70	69	86	55	64	63	72	64	75	65
Chile	63	65	54	52	58	48	58	44	66	55
Colombia	65	77	81	75	83	66			83	67
Mexico	63	59	68	62	58	57	46	67	72	71
Venezuela	57	53	40	51	44	59		42	47	

Adapted from Straubhaar, J., Fuentes, M., Abram, D., McCormick, P., Campbell, C., Youn, S. M., Inagaki, N., Wang, T. L., Ha, L., Shrikhande, S., Elasmar, M., Ahn, T. H., Chen, M. C., Clarke, S., and Takahashi, M. (2003, May). "Regional TV markets and TV program flows." Paper presented in the 2003 Conference of the International Communication Association. San Diego, California.

Table 5.4. Percentage of Prime Time and Global Time Per Day Occupied by U.S. Imports in Several Latin American Countries

	1962		1972		1982		1991		2001	
	Prime time	Global	Prime time	Global	Prime time	Global	Prime time	Global	Prime time	Global
Brazil	30	31	14	44	36	37	9	20	8	19
Chile	0	4	22	38	16	28	18	22	14	31
Colombia	31	18	11	10	14	23			13	21
Mexico	31	38	26	26	37	35	42	24	27	27
Venezuela	37	40	38	39	42	36			42	32

Adapted from Straubhaar, J., Fuentes, M., Abram, D., McCormick, P., Campbell, C., Youn, S. M., Inagaki, N., Wang, T. L., Ha, L., Shrikhande, S., Elasmar, M., Ahn, T. H., Chen, M. C., Clarke, S., and Takahashi, M. (2003, May). "Regional TV markets and TV program flows." Paper presented in the 2003 Conference of the International Communication Association. San Diego, California.

Table 5.5. Percentage of Foreign Programs in Mexican Open TV by Genre

Study	Year	Fiction	Variety	News	Sports	Cities Sampled
Crovi (1995a)	1994	62	28	9	23	D.F.
Sánchez Ruiz (1996)	1995	77[1](60)[2]	37 (33)	6 (6)	11 (6)	D.F., Guadalajara, León, & Uruapan
Crovi & Vilar (1995)	1995	71	38	0	23	D.F.
Lozano & García (1995)	1995	89 (72)	6 (5)	6 (6)	23 (23)	Monterrey
Sánchez Ruiz (1995)	1995	74 (59)	41 (38)	7 (7)	16 (9)	Guadalajara
Lozano & Huerta (2001)	1999	47 (45)	16 (12)	0	28 (28)	D.F, Guadalajara, & Monterrey (4 weeks)
Martínez & Lozano (2003)	2003	(60)	(3)	(1)	(2)	Average of six weeks, one each month (January–June) of four national channels

[1] Percentage of foreign programming
[2] Percentage of U.S. programming

REFERENCES

Antola, L., and Rogers, E. (1984). "Television flows in Latin America." *Communication Research* 11(2), pp. 183–202.

Arroyo, A., López, G., and Vega, G. (2003, June). "Regímenes de propiedad y conglomerados de medios audiovisuales en el continente americano." Paper presented at the X Encuentro de la Asociación Mexicana de Investigadores de la Comunicación, Puebla, Puebla.

Beltrán, L. R. (1978). "TV etchings in the minds of Latin Americans: conservatism, materialism, and conformism." *Gazette* 24(1), pp. 61–85.

Beltrán, L. R., and Fox, E. (1980). *Comunicación dominada*. Mexico: ILET Nueva Imagen.

Biltereyst, Daniël. (1992). "Language and culture as ultimate barriers? An analysis of the circulation, consumption and popularity of fiction in small European countries." *European Journal of Communication* 7, pp. 517–540.

Biltereyst, D., and Meers, P. (2000). "The international *telenovela* debate and the contra-flow argument: A reappraisal." *Media, Culture and Society* 22, pp. 393–413.

Blanco, J. (1996). "Oferta de programas nacionales y extranjeros en medios televisivos y análisis de su exposición y consumo por alumnos de secundaria en la Ciudad de Irapuato." Master's thesis, Tecnológico de Monterrey, Campus Eugenio Garza Sada (Monterrey).

Brittos, V. (2005a). "Globo, transnationalização e capitalismo." In V. Cruz Brittos and C. Bolaño (eds.), *Rede Globo: 40 anos de poder e hegemonia*, pp. 131–154. São Paolo: Paulus.

——— (2005b). "A economia política da TV Brasileira no período pré-digitalização." In O. Jambeiro, V. Brittos, and A. Benevenuto (eds.), *Comunicação, hegemonia e contra-hegemonia*, pp. 67–91. Salvador, Bahia, Brazil: EDUFBA.

Brunetti, V. (1996). "Flujos interculturales en América Latina: exportación e importación de productos regionales: informe sobre la comunicación en el Paraguay." In J. Marques de Melo (ed.), *Identidades culturais Latino-Americanas em tempos de comunicação global*, pp. 65–86. Sao Paolo, Brazil: Instituto Metodista de Ensino Superior/UNESCO.

Caron, A., and Bélanger, P. (1993). "A reception study of American television products in Québec." In Roger de la Garde, William Gilsdorf, and Ilja Wechselmann (eds.), *Small nations, big neighbour*, pp. 25–64. London: John Libbey.

Cisneros Group of Companies (n.d.). Claxon Interactive Group. At www.cisneros.com/en/default.htm? (accessed September 1, 2005)>

Cobo, L. (2001, February 17). "Music television: A global status report, Latin America poised for music video growth." *Billboard* 113(7), pp. 1–2.

Colitt, R. (1998, March 24). "Venezuela´s unfolding television drama: CGC hopes programming will help it win Latin America's media war." *Financial Times.*

Covington, R. (1996, May 8). "Latin America: Television hotbed." *International Herald Tribune*, p. 15.

Curran, J. (1990). "The 'new revisionism' in mass communication research." *European Journal of Communication* 5(2–3), pp. 135–165.

Davis, L. L. (2003). "Cultural proximity on the air in Ecuador: National, regional television outperforms imported U.S. programming." In M. Elasmar (ed.), *The impact of international television: A paradigm shift*, pp. 111–132. Mahwah, N.J.: Lawrence Erlbaum.

De la Garde, R. (1993). "Dare we compare?" In Roger de la Garde, William Gilsdorf, and Ilja Wechselmann (eds.), *Small nations, big neighbour*, pp. 25–64. London: John Libbey.

De la Garza, Y. (1996). "Patrones de exposición y preferencias programáticas televisivas de los jóvenes de preparatoria de Monterrey y su área conurbada." Master's thesis, Tecnológico de Monterrey.

De la Peña, G. (1998). "Del imaginario internacional de jóvenes regiomontanos." *Comunicación y Sociedad* (33), pp. 119–170.

De Pablos, E. (2003, January 20–26). "New world disorder: Spain's players tread water on Latin American prod'n." *Variety*, pp. 27–28.

Díaz, R. (1995). "Oferta de mensajes televisivos extranjeros en Monterrey, N.L. y las preferencias programáticas de los jóvenes de secundaria." Master's thesis, Tecnológico de Monterrey, Campus Eugenio Garza Sada.

DIRECTV (n.d.). DIRECTV Latin America, LLC. At www.directvla.com/ (accessed September 10, 2005).

Dorfman, A. (1980). *Reader´s nuestro que estás en la tierra: Ensayos sobre el imperialismo cultural.* Mexico: Editorial Nueva Imagen.

Dorfman, A., and Mattelart, A. (1978). *Para leer al Pato Donald: Comunicación de masas y colonialismo.* Mexico: Siglo XXI.

Duarte, L. G. (1999). "The impact of regional trade pacts on foreign TV enterprises in Latin America." *Transnational Broadcasting Studies* (electronic journal) (3). At www.tbsjournal.com/Archives/Fall99/Articles3/Duarte/duarte.html.

—— (2005). "Pecado capital: a novela dos Marinho com a TV paga." In V. Cruz Brittos and C. Bolaño (orgs.), *Rede Globo: 40 anos de poder e hegemonia*, pp. 325–340. São Paolo: Paulus.

Figueroa, J. (1996). "Oferta y consumo de programas televisivos extranjeros: Un análisis de los alumnos de secundaria de la Ciudad de Mexico." Master's thesis, Tecnológico de Monterrey, Campus Eugenio Garza Sada.

García, R. A. (1997). "Preferencias programáticas locales, nacionales y extranjeras en el área metropolitana de Monterrey." Master's thesis, Tecnológico de Monterrey.

García Calderón, C. (1987). *Para conectarse a cablevisión.* Mexico: Ediciones El Caballito.

"Gotita de amor conquista a los televidentes en Venezuela." (2003, October 7). At www.televisa.com (accessed June 10, 2005).

Hoskins, C., Mirus, R., and Rozeboom, W. (1989). "U.S. television programs in the international market: Unfair pricing?" *Journal of Communication* 39(2), pp. 55–75.

Hopewell, J. (2001, March 5–11). "Pair pact on Spanish lingo lit pix." *Variety*, p. 36.

—— (2001, July 30–August 5). "Soaps reign in Spain." *Variety*, p. 32.

James, A. (2000, November 20–26). "Multithematiques buys Brazil channel." *Variety*, p. 39.

Lozano, J. C. (1995/1996). "Oferta y recepción de televisión extranjera en Mexico" {"Supply and reception of foreign television in Mexico"). *Comunicación y Sociedad* (25/26), pp. 259–284.

—— (1997). "U.S. media reception in the Mexican Northern border." In Emile McAnany and Kenton T. Wilkinson (eds.), *Mass media and free trade: NAFTA and the cultural industries*. Austin: University of Texas.

—— (2000). "Oferta y consumo de contenidos transnacionales en Mexico." *Revista de Estudios sobre las Culturas Contemporáneas, Epoca 2*, 6(12), pp. 111–126.

—— (2003, October). "Research on the supply and consumption of foreign television contents in Mexico." Paper presented in the Conference Global Fusion, University of Texas, Austin.

—— (2004). "Mexican research on the supply and consumption of foreign media contents in Mexico." Paper presented at the 54th Annual Conference of the International Communication Association (ICA), "Communication Research in the Public Interest," New Orleans, May 29, 2004.

Lozano, J. C., and García Nuñez de Cáceres, J. (1995). "Oferta de programación audiovisual extranjera en la televisión aérea de Monterrey, Nuevo León." In Delia Crovi Druetta (coord.), *Desarrollo de las industrias audiovisuales en Mexico y Canadá*. Mexico: Facultad de Ciencias Políticas y Sociales, UNAM.

Lozano, J. C., and Huerta, J. E. (2001). "La programación televisiva Mexicana de 1999 desde la perspectiva de la diversidad." *Anuario de Investigación de la Comunicación CONEICC 8*, pp. 153–196.

Mattelart, A. (1974). *La cultura como empresa multinacional*. Mexico: Era.

Morley, D. (1993). "Active audience theory: Pendulums and pitfalls." *Journal of Communication 43*(4), pp. 13–19.

Nordenstreng, K., and Varis, T. (1974). *Television traffic: A one-way street?* Paris: UNESCO Report, No. 70.

Pasquali, A. (1972). *Comunicación y cultura de masas*. 2nd ed. Caracas: Monte Ávila Editores.

"Profile: Brazilian television network preparing to launch its first prime-time soap opera for the U.S. Spanish-speaking television market." (2002, April 7). *Weekend All Things Considered*.

"Ranking del 21 de julio al 27 de julio 2003." (2003, July). At www.agb.com.ve/contenido/ranking-semanal-contenido.htm (accessed November 27, 2003).

Rebouças, E. (2005). *América Latina: um território pouco exploradoe ameaçador para a TV globo*. In V. Cruz Brittos and C. Bolaño (orgs.), *Rede globo: 40 anos de poder e hegemonia*, pp. 157–170. São Paolo: Paulus.

Sánchez Ruiz, E. (1994/95). "Cine, televisión y video: Hábitos de consumo fílmico en Guadalajara." *Comunicación y Sociedad 22/23*, pp. 147–184.

Santa Cruz, A., and Erazo, V. (1981). *Compropolitan*. Mexico: ILET-Editorial Nueva Imagen.

Sinclair, J. (2003). "The Hollywood of Latin America: Miami as a regional center in television trade." *Television and New Media 4*(3), pp. 211–229.

Straubhaar, J. (2003). "Choosing national TV: Cultural capital, language, and cultural proximity in Brazil." In M. G. Elasmar (ed.), *The impact of international television: A paradigm shift*, pp. 77–110. Mahwah, N.J.: Lawrence Erlbaum.

Straubhaar, J., Youn, S. M., Campbell, C., Champanie, K., Ha, L., Shrikhande, S., Elasmar, M., Ahn, T. H., Chen, M. C., Clarke, S., and Takahashi, M. (1994). "Mercados para la televisión regional y flujos de programas." *Estudios sobre las Culturas Contemporáneas 6*(18), pp. 115–150.

Straubhaar, J., Fuentes, M., Abram, D., McCormick, P., Campbell, C., Youn, S. M., Inagaki, N., Wang, T. L., Ha, L., Shrikhande, S., Elasmar, M., Ahn, T. H., Chen, M. C., Clarke, S., and Takahashi, M. (2003, May). "Regional TV markets and TV program flows." Paper presented at the 2003 Conference of the International Communication Association, San Diego, Calif.

Sutter, M. (2001, January 15–21). "Telenovelas still simmer." *Variety* 381(8), pp. 47–52.

—— (2001, March 26–April 1). "Weak signal: Digital shows promise, but cable creeps along." *Variety*, pp. 34–40.

—— (2001, May 21–27). "Movies matter the most." *Variety*, pp. 34–40.

"Top 5 por señal abierta" (2003, November). At www.ibope.com.ar (accessed November 27, 2003).

Varis, T. (1984). "The international flow of television programmes." *Journal of Communication* 34(1), pp. 143–152.

Zona Latina (2006, March). "IBOPE cable television ratings in multi-country, Argentina, Brazil, Chile, Colombia, Mexico and Peru." At www.zonalatina.com/Cable0603.htm (accessed May 22, 2006).

6

Australia: Media and Globalization

Alan Knight

News Corporation became the first fully globalized media consortium by detaching itself from the vestiges of its Australian corporate origins in 2004 and locating itself squarely in the top five hundred U.S. corporations. In less than half a century, Rupert Murdoch and his family transformed News from a regional Australian newspaper to a horizontally and vertically integrated multimedia giant that sold not just news but also marketed its cultural packages across the United States, Europe, Asia, and the Pacific. In this process, Australia, whose media were progressively dominated by News Corporation products including newspapers, cinema, music, cable television, and sport, became a consumer of these American-accented products. As a result, Australia moved from the center and source of News Corporation businesses to an increasingly remote corner of the corporate empire. This chapter considers how the growth of News Corporation and the globalization of its agendas have impacted Australian journalism, politics, and culture.

ACQUIRING SOFT POWER

Rupert Murdoch's media career was rooted in the earthy but ultimately establishment-dependent mores of Australian journalism. His father Keith's successful transition from foreign correspondent to senior newspaper management, had been buttressed by a series of alliances with conservative Australian politicians, culminating in his honorary membership of the feudal classes through the granting of a knighthood. Sir Keith managed Australian newspaper chains and sought share ownership of them. His untimely death in 1952 left 23-year-old Rupert with control of a single regional newspaper, the Adelaide *News*. But young Rupert also inherited ambition; to own what his father had grown. By the end of the 1950s, young Rupert had tentatively expanded his Adelaide-based company, News Limited, to include Sunday newspapers, a women's magazine, and radio. In 1964, Rupert Murdoch founded Australia's first national newspaper, the *Australian*, based initially in the national capital, Canberra, and with page templates distributed to regionally located presses by aircraft. While conceived as a liberal publication, the *Australian* shifted to the right with a series of editorial sackings that allowed political negotiations to enhance Murdoch's growing business empire. Editorial support for selected politicians was swiftly followed by government concessions and deregulation.

Australian biographer George Munster saw News's "dynamism" as fueled by taxpayer support. Writing more than two decades ago, Munster said that Murdoch's private dealings with politicians led to direct and profitable help from the public sector:

> Starting with television in Australia, he moved into airlines, gambling mineral and oil exploration. In these ventures, he is a concessionaire or [holds] positions allocated and protected by authority and subject to limited competition; in some of them he is a buyer from and seller to governments, a recipient of their guarantees and even a borrower from government agencies. Operating on the interface of business and the state and publishing News papers which read sermons to politicians from great heights and published exposes from low recesses, he has always avoided complications arising from that dual location. (Munster 1985, pp. 3–4)

Murdoch established a pattern of exercising editorial support for politicians who in turn favored News priorities. He was unique, in that he had the drive, discipline, and coordination to spread this practice across the globe. After prolonged political lobbying in Britain, he moved overseas with the acquisition in 1968 of the ailing London-based paper *News of the World*. He saw his editorial direction as intertwined with profitability:

> Since a paper's success or failure depends on an editorial approach, why shouldn't I interfere when I see a way to strengthen its approach. What am I supposed to do, sit idly by and watch a paper go down the drain, simply because I am not supposed to interfere? Rubbish! That's the reason the *News of the World* started to fade. There was no-one there to trim the fat and wrench it out of its editorial complacency. (Shawcross 1992, p. 76)

Murdoch was establishing himself at the information nexus of the rapidly globalizing economy.

MARKET DOMINANCE

In Australia, News's steady growth led to the 1987 purchase of the paper chain that Rupert's father had managed, the Herald and Weekly Times group. The acquisition allowed News more than 60 percent of Australia's metropolitan newspaper circulation, with competition eliminated in Brisbane, Adelaide, Darwin, and Hobart. The then–Labor Prime Minister, Bob Hawke, declined to implement antimonopoly legislation against what journalists saw as the most concentrated press ownership outside the old Soviet Union. Hawke's response was politically pragmatic, sectarian, and short-term in outlook; claiming that the Herald management had been "viciously anti-Labour" and Murdoch was unlikely to be worse (Shawcross 1992, p. 244).

As the international News's interests globalize and the corporation's interests focused on key markets such as Britain and then the United States, distance allowed Australian outlets a degree of independence. Control was exercised through key editorial appointments who reported regularly to the chief executive. Australian News editors were subjected to flying visits from Rupert himself. Brisbane writer Hugh Lunn (2001), a former *Australian* News staffer, claimed "the look and body language" of executives changed at the mention of Rupert's name. His account shows just how closely local editors were scrutinized:

> When Rupert hit town they became like a herd of wildebeest; first excited that they could be near him, then frightened that he wouldn't like what they had been doing, and, finally, they were drawn into a controlled, instinctive panic leading occasionally to their own destruction. Rupert's visit was a much, much bigger occasion for editors than if some other world figure, merely the Pope, say, came to appraise their work. The Pope might also have a large degree of infallibility, but he could only threaten their next life not this one. The Queen might bestow an honour on an editor, but not dishonour. Whereas Rupert would not hesitate to describe a paper as dull and boring, which meant that the Editor and his editors were dull and boring. Rupert would even notice the technical errors and small mistakes—if the pictures were taken from too far away, the feature was too long, the headline didn't fit, the use of capital letters was incorrect, and the inevitable spelling mistakes—which was what made him frightening. (Lunn 2001, p. 137)

Editorial lines were considered and often decided at annual international senior management conferences, where favored politicians attended by invitation. In this way, News Corporation papers in Australia could consistently reflect Rupert Murdoch's right-wing opinions. Jack Waterford, the editor-in-chief of the independently owned *Canberra Times*, claimed News publications' editorial views were "increasingly monolithic." "When his [Murdoch's] interests are clear . . . his newspapers not only speak with one voice, but increasingly that voice is shrill, sometimes hysterical, and the voice and the interests are increasingly those of the world citizen, not the Australian citizen with some yen for playing politics and keeping politicians on their toes."

Waterford wrote,

> much of his [Murdoch's] cat-and-mouse game with politicians, particularly in Britain and Australia, is focused on securing favours or fending off efforts to control or regulate him. In the U.S. he is deeply committed to the Republican Party and to George W. Bush, not necessarily because he agrees with Bush's foreign policy, but because of his and the party's opposition to regulation. There is nothing many free-marketeers like more than monopolies and privileged access to markets, and luckily the Bush Administration is also very good at dispensing favours. Murdoch's gratitude is primarily shown by the amazing Fox channel, about as reliable a source of news as Radio Pyongyang (2004, p. 2).

According to writer David McKnight (2004), Rupert Murdoch's influence had an ideological impact on Australia's national politics as his local flagship, the *Australian*, became the most consistent popularizer of "hard-line free-market economics." "Today the *Australian* employs some of the best journalists in Australia," McKnight wrote. "Its neo-conservative political line comes largely from its columnists, its leaders, its invited contributors." McKnight quoted Paul Kelly, the former editor-in-chief of the *Australian*, as admitting that "the *Australian* has established itself in the marketplace as a newspaper that strongly supports economic libertarianism."

CORPORATE CITIZEN MURDOCH

Rupert Murdoch surrendered his Australian passport in 1985 to become an American citizen. He did so to more effectively compete for U.S. television licenses. He said he was not severing any links with Australia, and the News Corporation retained its Australian registration for another twenty years. Each year Rupert, often accompanied by his elder son Lachlan or his other children would fly back to Adelaide to report to his Australian shareholders. In 2004, Murdoch told the Australian meeting that News, the largest private company on the Australian exchanges, would henceforth be domiciled in the United States:

> We undertook this move for one reason: to create greater value for our shareholders. For more than eighty years, the Company has proudly called Australia its home. It is where our Company was founded, nurtured and from where we get our entrepreneurial spirit. Australia is our spiritual home and

will remain so. But over the last two decades as more of the Company's revenues and profits have come from our U.S. based businesses, it has become increasingly clear to us that without a primary listing on the New York Stock Exchange and eligibility on the U.S. indices, our shareholders would never experience the full benefits of our achievements. (*News Corporation* 2004, p. 4)

The move, he claimed, would have no discernible impact on News's Australian operations. Rather it could enhance access to the U.S.$12 trillion U.S. capital market. The *Australian Financial Review* (owned by the rival Fairfax chain) noted that in 2003 Australian shareholders "gave Murdoch his first defeat in half a century," by rejecting increased executive options. "[W]ith News emigrating to America, that won't be a problem," it reported (AFR 2004). The *Australian* supportively editorialized that the shift should be "a trigger for national pride, rather than wailing." "Rather than gnashing our teeth over the loss of News Corp from the Australian Stock Exchange's benchmark index, we should be encouraging foreign investment and making sure the settings are right for a new generation of world-beating Australian companies to emerge" (*Australian* 2004, p. 14). In the interim, Australia's press would be overwhelmingly foreign-owned.

GLOBALIZATION AND AUSTRALIA

Globalization is frequently depicted in purely economic terms. According to Noam Chomsky, globalization sprouted during reconstruction following World War II, which saw the United States emerge as the dominant economic power, eclipsing or undermining the old European empires. Chomsky (2003) claimed the world economy was to be rebuilt if only so it could absorb U.S. manufacturing surpluses:

> The new global order was to be subordinated to the needs of the U.S. economy and subject to U.S. political control as much as possible. Imperial controls, especially the British, were to be dismantled while Washington extended its own regional systems in Latin America and the Pacific on the principle of . . . what was good for us [i.e., the U.S.] is good for the world. (p. 149)

This agenda, which included deregulation, deunionization, and privatization, pursued by successive U.S. administrations, was implemented through the International Monetary Fund. According to former World Bank executive Joseph Stiglitz, globalization was accelerated by computerized communications and faster transport:

> Fundamentally it is the closer integration of the countries and people of the world which has been brought about by the enormous reduction of costs of

transportation and communication, and the breaking down of artificial barriers to the flow of goods, services, capital, knowledge and (to a lesser extent) people across borders. (Stiglitz 2002, p. 9)

Yet, as the global economies evolved, communications became more than merely a facilitator of economic change. It became the product that sold itself. Australian expatriate journalist John Pilger claimed "global economy" had become a modern Orwellian term, extolling lifestyles that were unachievable by most of the world's population:

> Central to this business state are the media conglomerates, which have unprecedented power, owning press and television, book publishing, film production and databases. They provide a virtual world of the 'eternal present', as *Time* magazine called it; politics by media, war by media, justice by media, even grief by media (Princess Diana). The 'global economy' is their most important media enterprise.

Australia had a long history of enthusiastically barracking for empires, both virtual and concrete. It was a proud member of the British Empire, sending volunteers for a series of imperial wars, including the Sudan expedition, the Boer War, World War I, and the interventions against the embryonic Soviet Union. World War II was a turning point. The front-page reports of Japan's destruction of the Britain's Far East fleet eclipsed imperial propaganda depicting Australia as a safe colonial haven. The subsequent fall of Singapore to Japanese forces in 1942, severed imperial transport and communications links to the southern dominions. The now-isolated Australian government turned across the Pacific for support, embracing a new military protector, the United States. The thousands of GIs who subsequently came to Australia to fight the war in the Pacific arena introduced Australians to a democratic culture of consumerism, from Coca Cola to Hollywood, sparking a fifty-year Australian progression from curtseying to the British Royal Family to joining an audience with the *Simpsons*.

Australia returned the favor by sending troops to support the United States in the Korean and Vietnam wars.

THE AUSTRALIAN SHERIFF

The Australian Prime Minister John Howard had been visiting the United States when Osama bin Laden's terrorists forced aircraft into the World Trade Center. What had been intended to be a ritualized homage to the U.S. links became a call to arms as the United States activated long-standing military agreements.

Three days after the 9/11 attacks, the U.S. Congress gave President George Bush a mandate to pursue terrorists with "all necessary and appropriate force" (Bacevich 2002, p. 237). President Bush subsequently proceeded with a policy of unilateralism, where U.S. supremacy was globally declared to be permanent and universal. Even allies were challenged to be either with the United States "or with the terrorists." Noam Chomsky (2003) saw this adoption of unilateralism as the abandonment of any pretense of observing international consensus. The 9/11 attacks were significant, in his view, because the Twin Towers were not located in a small and relatively powerless state: "For the first time, an attack on the rich and powerful countries succeeded on a scale that is regrettably not unfamiliar to their traditional domains" (p. 209).

Australia's political place in this new world order was defined by President Bush when he described the Australian Prime Minister John Howard as a regional "sheriff." President Bush had been asked whether he saw Australia as a "deputy sheriff" in Southeast Asia. The U.S. president replied, "No. We don't see it as a deputy sheriff. We see it as a sheriff" (CNN 2003).

U.S.–based financial historian Nial Ferguson (2004) saw the Bush government's post-9/11 unilateralism as a historical development similar to that of the nineteenth century British Empire globally deploying its power to depose despots, encourage trade, and institute sound governance (pp. 24–25). He claimed the United States was running an empire, albeit a liberal one, in denial. Ferguson said the contemporary United States exercised imperial power through both military interventions such as Iraq and through "soft power" such as cultural exports. The United States used local elites to secure its aims:

> It is primarily concerned with its own security and maintaining international communications and, secondarily, with ensuring access to raw materials (principally) but not exclusively oil. It is also in the business of providing a limited number of public goods; peace, by intervening against some bellicose regimes and in some civil wars; freedom of the seas and skies for trade; and a distinctive form of "conversion," usually called Americanization, which is carried out less by old style Christian missionaries than by the exporters of American consumer goods and entertainment. Its methods of formal rule are primarily military in character; its methods of informal rule rely heavily on non-governmental organisations and corporations and, in some cases, local elites. (Ferguson 2004, p. 13)

Under this world order, Washington and Canberra appeared to be renewing old attachments, in which Australia was the regional standard bearer for Western interests. In nineteenth-century literature, imperial presumptions frequently constructed indigenous societies as poorly governed, denying local goods to imperial markets, and subject to infiltration by foreign interests (Dixon 1995, pp. 118–133). New Guinea, Fiji, and even New Zealand had been acquired by the Crown with Australian support. Threatening foreigners were then described as French, Russian, or German: Britain's imperial competitors. Today the threat is globalized. The enemies requiring metropolitan intervention now are simply those declared "terrorists" by the United States. The rationale for intervention is also familiar; indigenous populations need guidance in governance, so that communications, trade, and investment might be protected.

In the twenty-first century, Australia might be seen as an exponent of "soft power," exercising media and economic influence on behalf of the United States on notionally independent Pacific microstates.

OWNING LOCALLY, THINKING GLOBALLY

In News Corporation's 2004 annual report, Rupert Murdoch said the News had set the standard for how a media company in the twenty-first century should look:

> Our assets are global, with operations across five continents. Our assets are *diversified*, encompassing businesses that create content and those that distribute that content. Our assets are *balanced*, between those whose revenues are dependent on advertising and those that are not. And our assets are of *varying maturities*, neatly divided between those generating significant profits today and those positioned to deliver growth tomorrow. (News Corporation 2004)

In Australia, a country with a population of about twenty million people, News controls more than one hundred national, metropolitan, suburban, regional, and Sunday papers. These include the largest-circulation daily, the *Herald Sun*, and the second-biggest-selling newspaper, the *Sunday Mail*. News owns Australia's leading music publisher, Festival Mushroom, and the local branch of the international book publisher, HarperCollins. It effectively controls the National Rugby League, a popular football code that generates endless breathless copy for sports writers for News publications including the *Big League*. It holds a major share in the major cable television network Foxtel, which carried the familiar international News products *Fox News*, *Sky Movies*, and *Sky Sports*. Meanwhile, News executives are lobbying to remove regulations that stop newspaper owners from also controlling terrestrial radio and television networks. Opinions are gathered and informed by Newspoll, the polling company used by newspapers to determine the success and failure of Australian politicians and their policies.

Perhaps, however, it is Fox Studios that best signifies Murdoch's diversified, globalized philosophy, integrating content and distribution, while underpinning commercial interests with tacit government subsidies. Located near the heart of Sydney, the production studio, which opened in 1998, includes a theme park, shops selling Fox promotional products, a shopping center, and a cinema complex. The New South Wales state government allowed the studio's construction on what had been the state agricultural showgrounds, for a century the site of the Royal Easter Show, a state fair that attracted more than a million patrons each year. The state government relocated the Easter Show, in the hope that Fox Studios might use relatively cheap Australian film crews to undercut Hollywood and produce movies for its international network. In doing so, it prioritized transnational corporate cultural products over a traditional event organized by a local association.

The Matrix Trilogy, a series of science fiction films about an information network fed by isolated and powerless consumers, was among the first major movies shot at Fox Studios. Starring the Lebanon-born Canadian citizen Keanu Reeves, the international blockbuster movies featured a supporting cast of Australian actors who adopted American accents to conform to the demands of the U.S. domestic market. Internationally known Sydney locations such as the Opera House were kept off camera to maintain the illusion that globally marketed cultural products were essentially *American*.

The U.S. cultural dominance of the Australian cinema box office is overwhelming. Two hundred U.S. films were released in Australia in 2004, representing 63 percent of films offered to the public. Yet, American films took 85.9 percent of the total box office. There were no Australian films in the fifty highest-grossing films in Australia in 2004. The most popular film, *Shrek 2*, an animated medieval fairy tale, was voiced by improbable yet familiar American accents. Film number fifty, *Man on Fire*, a Fox film, depicted a former American agent murdering corrupt Mexican police officials, as he delivered American-style justice, which ignored Mexican sovereignty.

In the same year, the Australian film industry released twelve feature films and four documentaries. None of these films impact the American market. Indeed in Australia, *Man on Fire* grossed almost AUS$1 million more than the most popular Australian film, *Strange Bedfellows*, a comedy featuring Paul Hogan, whose international reputation was established by the caricatured Australian bushman Crocodile Dundee.

CULTIVATING AN AUSTRALIAN ACCENT

Australians' primary alternative to the cross-marketed Murdoch packages is the Australian Broadcasting Corporation (ABC). The ABC is in

many ways the antithesis of the News group; a regulated, state owned
and heavily unionized content producer and distributor.

Founded as a radio broadcaster in 1932 and patterned on the British
Broadcasting Commission, ABC broadcasts are notably anglophone, with
announcers mimicking British upper-class pronunciations:

> Opening day programs included the first *Children's Session* with Bobby
> Bluegum, the first sports program, *Racing Notes* with W A Ferry calling the
> Randwick races, *British Wireless News* received by cable from London,
> weather, stock exchange and shipping news, the ABC Women's Associa-
> tion session (topics were "commonsense housekeeping" and needlecraft),
> a talk on goldfish and their care, Morning Devotions, and music. (ABC
> 2005c)

The ABC was in 2004 one of Australia's most important content
providers; offering the nation's largest electronic journalism output, six
major radio networks, national and international television networks,
music and press publishing, and new (online) media.

The ABC transmitted its programs via 973 terrestrial analogue television transmitters and 949 radio transmitters. Outside Australia, ABC Asia
Pacific reached Australia's neighbors via Panamsat 2 and 8. Radio Australia continued to be delivered by shortwave using both terrestrial stations and satellites ("ABC Programs" 2004, p. 6). Meanwhile, ABC Consumer Publishing released what it described as "800 consumer products
relating to ABC programming and Charter activities " in 2003–2004. These
included cookbooks, magazines, fiction, DVDs of local production, and
even an "MP3-CD consumer product" that allowed an audio CD to contain up to ten hours of audio book recording (ABC 2004b, p. 73). These
were marketed through 39 ABC shops. In doing so the ABC generated
AUS$8.19 million in profits.

Also in 2004, ABC Online received an average of 14.9 million page ac-
cesses each month. Over a quarterly period, the number of Australians
visiting ABC Online was 2.4 million, a reach of 23.6 percent of all those online each quarter (ABC 2004b, p. 24).

As a public broadcaster, the ABC sought to educate as well as entertain
and inform. Speaking to the Australian Industry group in 2004, the ABC
Chair Donald McDonald said that "Public broadcasting might be seen either as a post-Enlightenment project, or part of the Victorian mission of
public education." He outlined the essential differences between the ABC
and the commercial content providers:

> To accuse our commercial colleagues of not using television's enormous po-
> tential for anything other than entertainment would be pointless. We would
> be accusing them of breaking a promise they never made. It's nowhere in the

commercial broadcaster's contract. But it is in ours. The ABC acts as the counterpoint to the commercial profit motive—the social profit motive. That's what sets us apart. That's what makes us worth having. And we don't just give time to public affairs programming—peak time, right in the heart of the schedule—but we give quality to it as well. Yet, for all that, the ABC—if not exalted—is at least tolerated and funded. (McDonald 2004)

The ABC's charter, monitored by annual reports to parliament, requires that the ABC be balanced and distinctively Australian. The *Australian Broadcasting Corporation Act of 1983* demands the ABC broadcast "programs that contribute to a sense of national identity and inform and entertain, and reflect the cultural diversity of, the Australian community" (ABC 2005a). Further, the ABC is required to prove these claims to Parliament, as it attempts to do in the following excerpt from its 2004 annual report:

The distinctiveness of ABC programs and services is demonstrated through qualities such as its genre mix, spread of services throughout Australia and internationally, level and mix of Australian content, and recognition through awards and peer review. Eighty-three per cent of Newspoll respondents believe the ABC does a good job in being distinctively Australian and contributing to national identity. The Corporation extended further its regional radio services with the opening of its 60th local radio station in Erina, New South Wales. . . . Internationally the Corporation continued to extend its presence and profile in the region. Radio Australia increased its shortwave transmissions by 15 percent to 200 hours per day and ABC Asia Pacific is now received in 32 countries across the Asia Pacific region ("International broadcasting" 2004, p. 62). At home, ABC Television reported a decline of 4 percent to 48 percent in the level of Australian content broadcast between 6am and midnight. ("ABC television" 2004, p. 49)

However, distinctively Australian the ABC claimed to be in the new millennium, old cultural habits died hard. The ABC's lingering attachment to British manners and processes may be reflected by the appointment of the Queen's press secretary, Geoff Crawford, as director of corporate affairs. His corporate marketing unit manages the ABC brand, including partnerships, cross-promotions, community events, and cross-divisional marketing needs (Crawford 2004, p. 88). It might seem that at least somewhere in the national broadcaster's back corridors, Britannia still rules the airwaves!

WOODSTOCK IS DEAD

In February 2005, the conservative national government appointed right-wing *Australian* columnist Janet Albrechtsen as an ABC board member.

The appointment sharply highlighted the divide in philosophy, governance, and application between the Murdoch-led media transnational and the taxpayer-funded national broadcaster.

The ABC was governed by a Ministry-appointed board of directors whose powers and responsibilities were vested in the *Australian Broadcasting Corporation Act of 1983*. The act defined the functions of the corporation as contributing to a sense of national identity, broadcasting educational material, encouraging international awareness of Australia, and informing Australians about the rest of the world.

Albrechtsen had previously attacked the ABC for what she called its "left-wing bias," even claiming the staff-elected member of the board was "a remnant of the Soviet-style workers' collective," suggesting that election rather than appointment to the board was a result of an anachronistic, authoritarian, worker-oriented communist system (*Australian* 2004). Her appointment was hailed, however, in the *Australian* by former conservative communications minister Neil Brown, who saw Albrechtsen as seeking "balance," which in his view, the ABC lacked. He cited as evidence his belief that "the official ABC position is, first of all, against anything American":

> On the ABC, all industry is bad, all chemicals are poisonous, all wilderness is pristine, all animals are gentle, all business is evil and all government is a conspiracy. Frankly, I couldn't care less whether they are right or wrong. All I want is some balance and that is what we have not been getting. (*Australian* 2005)

Brown predicted Albrechtsen's appointment to the ABC board would create a backlash. Sweeping aside critics in a style reminiscent of Fox News, Brown said Albrechtsen would "cause a real stir in the ranks of the intelligentsia." "The luvvies and the bleeding hearts won't like it," Brown predicted.

Albrechtsen, meanwhile, said that eliminating bias from the ABC would be her major priority on the board. She had previously described "media bias as a subtle beast." "Bias shows in things like story selection and interviewee selection," she said. "It has to do with how, for example, news suits the ABC's anti-Bush agenda."

To examine how this definition of bias might apply to her own work, I examined forty-eight Albrechtsen opinion pieces of one thousand words each, published in the *Australian* in 2004. Thirty-five percent of these articles could be considered antilabor, with the social democratic Labour Party seen as being intertwined with unionism: The left had grown old but not grown up, she said. "[T]imes have changed, the world has moved on and fewer and fewer people want to join their party. Woodstock is dead" (*Australian* 2004). Union campaigns to recognize workplace stress was turning Australia into a "cry baby country" (*Australian* December 29, 2004). One article did praise the Labour Party, but only when former Labour leader Mark Latham appeared to embrace conservative family values, similar to those espoused by President Bush or Australian Prime Minister John Howard (*Australian* February 4, 2004); however, her views on Latham hardened, particularly after he called her a "skanky ho" (a prostitute). She in turn referred to the opposition leader as "princess" (*Australian* July 7, 2004).

In contrast, the conservative leader John Howard was, according to Albrechtsen, preferred "by the rest of us." "We're glad to be conservative," she wrote, explicitly endorsing an identified political philosophy:

> Conservatism creeps up on you without you even knowing it. That's what frightens the left so and why they have comprehensively failed to challenge it. And a media screeching about dumb and duped voters only cements conservatism's future. (*Australian* October 13, 2004)

Albrechtsen was also strongly supportive of Howard's mentor, George Bush. The U.S. President was described as a "man of action." "Not for Bush, diplomatic inaction, the preferences for tokens over genuine actions or the mawkish sympathies endemic to Western politics," she wrote (*Australian* November 3, 2004). Fourteen percent of her columns in 2004, strongly supported the invasion of Iraq. The "media frenzy" over the torturing of prisoners at Abu Ghraib betrayed media bias, she said. "With photos in hand and under the seductive theme of the public's right to know, many of the media showed the images again and again. . . . [I]t is less enthused about addressing its own culpability for the violence that publishing these images may generate" (*Australian* May 9, 2004).

Twenty-five percent of Albrechtsen's columns might be seen as fitting a consistent right-wing agenda. The liberal, openly homosexual High Court Judge Michael Kirby was claimed to be undermining the law by attempting to meld the roles of judge and crusader for change. Kirby was treading a "well worn path, pointing to so-called fundamental human rights, as laid down by a bunch of international laws" (*Australian* October 20, 2004). Meanwhile, supporting gay marriages was seen as "moral relativism, where all lifestyles are seen as equal" (*Australian* May 12, 2004). Feminists or "femocrats" were "1970s gender trippers"; "They talk about liberating women but continue to deride or ignore women who choose to stay at home and care for children" (*Australian* December 8, 2004).

Globalization was good, particularly if it meant free trade with the United States of America. Critics such as the Greens were dismissed as peddling gloom (*Australian* February 11, 2004). The Greens were else-where called "our very own lodestar to lunacy" with their leader Bob Brown curiously described as "radioactive." Offshoring Australian jobs to developing countries was better than charity:

> The Internet revolution has allowed people in India and China to lift them-selves out of poverty and even move into the middle classes by doing jobs for companies in the West for a fraction of the price that employees back home will do them. Whether its call centres, credit card processing or infor-mation technology work by software engineers, white collar jobs are on the move. (*Australian* December 5, 2004)

BIAS IS A SUBTLE BEAST

Albrechtsen fails her own definition of bias: She privileged the familiar leaders of the right, such as President Bush or Prime Minister Howard, whilst lampooning or vilifying those that she saw as of the left, in partic-ular the Australian Labor Party, its affiliated unions, the Greens and envi-ronmentalists. Like most *Australian* columnists, she selected issues that fell within themes familiar throughout News Corporation's international operations; conservative social values, deregulation, antiunionism, priva-tization, and of course globalization.

However, as a board member of the ABC, Albrechtsen is required by legislation to maintain the independence and integrity of the corporation. She also must ensure that the news and information gathering and pre-sentation by the corporation is accurate and impartial according to the recognized standards of impartial journalism. It would seem to follow that she would be required to eliminate at the ABC, the sort of journalism she pursues at News Corporation where no such charter existed.

Further, as a former communications minister, Neil Brown should have known that the ABC, by legislation, was precluded from having an offi-cial ABC position against anything American. Brown's other unsubstanti-ated claims, if made by an ABC employee, could be seen to be in breach of the ABC charter and subject to ministerial scrutiny. However, Brown was writing for News Corporation, whose columnists appeared to be ul-timately responsible only to an American citizen, Rupert Murdoch. Brown's support for Albrechtsen should not be seen as a move to eradi-cate bias at the ABC but rather as a protest against the ABC including voices with which Brown disagreed. Indeed, he appeared to endorse the journalism of intolerance and exclusion often promoted by News Corpo-ration opinion writers.

TRANSNATIONALIZING AUSTRALIA

Australia began its life as a convict colony, established as a depository for criminals who might have been bound for North America had it not been for George Washington's revolution. Cultural imperialism, as practiced in eighteenth-century London, was in that sense, strictly a one-way trip to the other end of the world. But two hundred years of hemispherical separation allowed Australia to develop a nationalistic culture, which began to question British dominance. The nationalist Australian Labour Party and in particular the anti-imperial union movement, played key roles in demanding an independent national identity. British institutions such as the BBC, seeded Australian counterparts, such as the ABC, which grew to promote unique Australian characteristics.

Meanwhile, as the British Empire ebbed away, the habit of intellectual, social, and military dependence on an imperial power shifted toward the United States. This shift, which Australian nationalists called a "cultural cringe," was enhanced by the new communications technologies, which enabled globalization. This shift was ultimately realized with President Bush's post-9/11 declaration of American global supremacy.

John Pilger recognized that the globalization of American interests was powered by media conglomerates, which profited from the deregulation of national economies and the Americanization of local cultures. News Corporation, which began as an Australian company, also appeared to see globalization in this way, by transporting itself to the United States, where the financial power that created the News's virtual empire resided. Rupert Murdoch saw this move as setting the standard for transnational media companies in the twenty-first century. But while he may depict himself as a man of the world, Murdoch has securely relocated himself. As an American citizen, he lives just up the road from Washington.

APPENDIX: AUSTRALIAN NEWS CORPORATIONS AND HOLDINGS

APN NEWS AND MEDIA

Chairman/CEO
James Parkinson (Chairman)
Minor Newspapers
20 regional newspapers
Outdoor
Adshel
APN Outdoor

Australian Posters
Buspak
Captive Media
Cody
TaxiMedia
Tribe
Broadcasting
4KQ Brisbane
5DN Adelaide

Summary of Australian News Corporations Holdings

Corporation	Metro Newspapers	Minor Newspapers	Magazines	Outdoor	Broadcasting	Film	Cable	Television	Satellite Television	Books	Other Assets
APN News and Media		×		×	×		×				×
Australian Broadcasting Corporation			×		×			×		×	
DMG Radio Australia					×						
John Fairfax Holdings Ltd	×	×	×								×
News Limited	×	×	×			×	×	×	×	×	×
Prime Television Ltd								×			
Publishing & Broadcasting Ltd (PBL)			×					×			×
Rural Press Limited	×	×			×						
Seven Network			×					×			×
Southern Cross Broadcasting Australia Ltd					×			×	×		×
Telstra Corporation Ltd							×				×
Ten Group Ltd						×		×			
Village Roadshow Ltd					×			×			×
West Aust. Newspapers Holdings Ltd	×	×									
WIN Corporation Pty. Ltd					×			×			×

Australian Radio Network
Gold FM Melbourne
Mix 101.1 FM Melbourne
Mix 102.3 FM Adelaide
Mix 106.5 FM Sydney
New 97.3 FM Brisbane
NewstalkeZB
Nova 93.7FM Perth
The Edge 96.1 FM Sydney
The Radio Network
WSFM Sydney
Cable
World Movies

AUSTRALIAN BROADCASTING CORPORATION

Chairman/CEO
Donald McDonald AO (Chairman)
Magazines
ABC Magazines:
jmag
limelight Magazine
Organic Gardener
Saddle Club Magazine
Funtime with Friends
Rollercoaster
Delicious
Broadcasting
ABC Radio Network
ABCNewsRadio Network
Triple J Network
Classic FM Network
Radio National Network
Local Radio Network (60 stations)
Radio Australia Network
Message Stick - Indigenous
51 regional radio stations
Television
ABC Channel 2 Television Service
ABC 2
(1 national analogue; 2 digital services
   with 97 transmitters Australia-wide)
KidsTV
Message Stick - Indigenous
ABC AsicPacific

Local television in each state
Books
ABC Books
Other Assets
ABC Online (abc.net.au)
ABC NewsOnline
Message Stick Online - Indigenous
ABC Shop (39 shops)
abcshop.com.au
ABC Contemporary Music
ABC DVD
ABC Video
ABC Classics
ABC Audio
ABC Broadband News
ABC NewMedia Service
ABC Digital Service
dig (a music-based service via Internet
   and digital television)

DMG RADIO AUSTRALIA

Chairman/CEO
R. Gilbert (Chairman)
Broadcasting
5 metropolitan radio licenses
60 regional radio licenses

JOHN FAIRFAX HOLDINGS LTD

Chairman/CEO
Dean Wills AO (Chairman)
Metro Newspapers
The Sydney Morning Herald
The Sun-Herald
The Age
The Sunday Age
Minor Newspapers
60 regional and community newspa-
   pers
Magazines
Good Weekend
Television
Sunday Life
the (Sydney) magazine
theage (Melbourne) magazine

Uncorked
Drive
Fashion
The Australian Financial Review
The Australian Financial Review
  (Weekend Edition)
AFR Magazine
Boss
Business Review Weekly
Personal Investor
Asset
Shares
CFO Australia
MIS Australia
Other Assets
smh.com.au
theage.com.au
rugbyheaven.com
realfooty.com.au
moneymanager.com.au
tradingroom.com.au
mycareer.com.au
domain.com.au
drive.com.au
cracker.com.au
AAP Information Services (43.4%)
afr.com

NEWS LIMITED

Chairman/CEO
Rupert Murdoch (Chairman)
Metro Newspapers
The Australian
The Courier-Mail
Daily Telegraph
Herald Sun
The Advertiser
The Mercury
Gold Coast Bulletin
The Sunday Mail
The Sunday Telegraph
NT News
Sunday Herald Sun
Sunday Mail
Sunday Tasmanian
Sunday Territorian

Sunday Times
Weekly Times
Minor Newspapers
About 100 regional and suburban
  newspapers
Magazines
Big League
InsideOut
donna hay
Film
Fox Studios Australia
Cable
Fox Movie Channel
Fox News Channel
Fox Sports Australia (50%)
FX
National Geographic Channel -
  (Worldwide)
Television
Fox Sports Australia
FOXTEL (50%)
Premier Movie Partnership (20%) (Aust
  & NZ)
Satellite Television
FOXTEL (25%)
Books
HarperCollins Publishers
Other Assets
Festival Records
Mushroom Records
National Rugby League
News Interactive

PRIME TELEVISION LTD

Chairman/CEO
Paul Ramsey (Chairman)
Television
8 regional television licenses

PUBLISHING & BROADCASTING LTD (PBL)

Chairman/CEO
James Packer (Chairman)
Magazines
Australian Consolidated Press

Women's Weekly
Woman's Day
Dolly
NW
TV Week
Cleo
Harpers Bazaar, Belle
Gourmet Traveller
House and Garden
Cosmopolitan
The Bulletin
Wheels
Television
Nine Network
Other Assets
Crown (entertainment venue)
Burswood International Resort Casino
FOXTEL (25%)
SkyNews (33%)
Sydney Super Dome
Hoyts
Ticketek
ninemsm
seek.com.au
PremierMediaGroup

RURAL PRESS LIMITED

Chairman/CEO
John B. Fairfax (Chairman)
Metro Newspapers
Canberra Times
Minor Newspapers
150 regional newspapers
Broadcasting
5 radio licenses in South Australia
1 radio license in Ipswich, Qld.

SEVEN NETWORK

Chairman/CEO
Kerry Stokes (Chairman)
Magazines
Total Girl
K-Zone
Home Beautiful

New Idea
Marie Claire
Better Homes
Men's Health
Family Circle
Your Garden
That's Life
Girlfriend
TV Hits
Golf Leisure
Lifestyle
Television
Seven Network (Channel 7)
Other Assets
Ticketmaster7
Telstra Dome

SOUTHERN CROSS BROADCASTING AUSTRALIA LTD

Chairman/CEO
J. C. Dahlsen (Chairman)
Broadcasting
2UE Sydney
3AW Melbourne
MAGIC 693
4BC Qld.
4BH Qld.
6PR
96FM
Sky Radio
Television
Channel 9 Adelaide
Southern Cross Ten Qld.
Southern Cross Ten Northern NSW
Southern Cross Ten Southern NSW
Southern Cross Ten VIC
Southern Cross Ten Darwin
Southern Cross Ten Central
Southern Cross Ten Tasmania
Central GTS/BKN
Satellite Television
Satellite Decoder Registration

Other Assets
Southern Cross Syndication
Southern Cross Radio Monitoring
Southern Cross Telecommunications

TELSTRA CORPORATION LTD

Chairman/CEO
Bob Mansfield (Chairman)
Cable
FOXTEL (50%)
Other Assets
Big Pond Internet services

TEN GROUP LTD

Chairman/CEO
Izzy Asper (Chairman of CanWest
  Global Communications)
Television
Ten Network (Ten)

VILLAGE ROADSHOW LTD

Chairman/CEO
John R. Kirby (Chairman)
Broadcasting
10 metropolitan radio licenses
2 regional radio licenses
Film
Village Roadshow Pictures
Roadshow Films

Television
Roadshow Television
Other Assets
Roadshow Entertainment
Warner Bros. Movie World
Sea World
Wet 'N Wild Water World
Warner Roadshow Movie World Studios
Sea World Nara Resort

WEST AUST. NEWSPAPERS HOLDINGS LTD

Chairman/CEO
W. G. Kent (Chairman)
Metro Newspapers
The West Australian Newspaper
Minor Newspapers
19 regional newspapers

WIN CORPORATION PTY. LTD

Chairman/CEO
Bruce Gordon (Chairman)
Broadcasting
i98FM radio
C91.3 FM radio
Television
WIN TV Digital Transmission
Crawfords Australia
Other Assets
WinNET

REFERENCES

"ABC programs and services: Transmission" (2004). In *Australian Broadcasting Corporation annual report*, p. 6. At www.abc.net.au/corp/annual_reports/ar04/pdf/ABC_AR_03-04_part1.pdf (accessed January 23, 2006).

"ABC television" (2004). In *Australian Broadcasting Corporation annual report*, p. 49. At www.abc.net.au/corp/annual_reports/ar04/pdf/ABC_AR_03-04_part3.pdf (accessed January 23, 2006).

Australian Broadcasting Corporation (2005a). ABC act, charter, and policy documents. At http://abc.net.au/corp/charter.htm (accessed February 28, 2005).

———— (2005b). "ABC Enterprises." At http://abc.net.au/corp/pubs/enterprises.pdf (accessed February 28, 2005).

—— (2005c). "About the ABC: History of the ABC, the birth of the ABC." At www.abc.net.au/corp/history/hist2.htm (accessed January 23, 2006).

Australian Film Commission (2005, January 27). "Australian films' 2004 box office share." At www.afc.gov.au/newsandevents/mediarelease/2005/release_350.aspx (accessed January 23, 2006).

Bacevich, A. (2002). *American empire: The realities and consequences of U.S. diplomacy.* London: Harvard Press.

Browning, J. (2002). *Dynasties.* Sydney: ABC Books.

Chenoweth, N. (2001). *Virtual Murdoch: Reality wars on the information highway.* London: Secker and Warburg.

Chomsky, N. (2003). *Hegemony or survival: America's quest for global dominance.* New York: Metropolitan Books.

Crawford, Geoff (2004). *Australian Broadcasting Corporation annual report,* p. 84. At www.abc.net.au/corp/annual_reports/ar04/pdf/ABC_AR_03-04_part3.pdf (accessed January 23, 2006).

Dixon, R. (1995). *Writing the colonial adventure: Race, gender and nation in Anglo-Australian popular fiction, 1875–1914.* Cambridge: Cambridge University.

Evans, H. (1983). *Good* Times, *bad* Times. London: Weidenfeld and Nicholson.

Ferguson, N. (2004). *Colossus: The price of America's empire.* New York: Penguin.

"Fox Entertainment Group information." At www.foxtel.com.au (accessed January 27, 2005).

Freedman, C. (1994). *Citizen Murdoch: A case study in the paradox of economic efficiency.* Kensington: University of New South Wales, School of Economics.

Greenwald, R. (2004). *Outfoxed: Rupert Murdock's war on journalism.* New York: Disinformation Co.

"International broadcasting" (2004). In *Australian Broadcasting Corporation annual report,* p. 62. At www.abc.net.au/corp/annual_reports/ar04/pdf/ABC_AR_03-04_part3.pdf (accessed January 23, 2006).

Kiernan, T. (1986). *Citizen Murdoch.* New York: Dodd, Mead.

Leapman, M. (1984). *Barefaced cheek: Rupert Murdoch.* UK: Coronet.

Lewis, S., and McDonald, A. (2005, February 25). "Labor cries 'cronyism' over ABC appointment." *Australian,* p. 4.

Lunn, H. (2001). *Working for Rupert.* Sydney: Hodder.

Marjoribanks, T. K. (2000). *News Corporation, technology and the workplace: Global strategies, local change.* Melbourne: Cambridge University.

McDonald, Donald. (2004). Speech to the Australian Industry group, text online at www.abc.net.au/corp/pubs/speeches/s1173202.htm.

McKnight, D. (2004, February). "Rupert Murdoch and the culture war." *Australian Book Review.* At home.vicnet.net.au/~abr/Feb04/McKnight.htm (accessed January 15, 2006).

Melvern, L. (1988). *The end of the street.* London: Methuen.

Munster, G. (1985). *A paper prince.* Ringwood, Victoria, Australia: Viking.

News Corporation Ltd. (1980 and 2004). *News Corporation Limited annual report.*

Page, B. (2003). *The Murdoch archipelago.* London: Simon and Schuster.

Pilger, J. (2002). *The new rulers of the world.* London: Verso.

Powell, D. (1991). *News on news: A report on how News Corporation Limited covers itself.* Broadway: Australian Centre for Independent Journalism.

Prestowitz, C. (2003). *Rogue nation*. New York: Basic Books.

Regan, S. (1976). *Rupert Murdoch: A business biography*. London: Angus and Robertson.

Shawcross, W. (1992). *Rupert Murdoch: Ringmaster of the information circus*. London: Chatto & Windus.

Stiglitz, J. (2002). *Globalization and its discontents*. London: Penguin Books.

Tuccille, J. (1990). *Murdoch: A biography*. London: Piatkus.

Viking News Corporation annual report (2004). At www.newscorp.com.au (accessed January 27, 2005).

Waterford, J. (2004, August 21). "Flaws in the Murdoch empire." *Canberra Times*, p. 2.

7

The Corporate Model from National to Transnational

Lee Artz

As the contributions to this collection indicate, the corporate media and their specific projects around the globe undergo frequent realignment subject to the vagaries of the media market and political changes internationally and within various nation-states. Indeed, the details of various media joint ventures, direct foreign investments, or mergers will likely be dated before the publication of this book. Nonetheless, the model of media deregulation, privatization, and commercialization so clearly demonstrated here characterizes media practices everywhere—from the smallest radio station in Africa to the declining public broadcasting systems everywhere—even as community and independent media projects (e.g., from the international journal *Le Monde Diplomatiqué* and Pacific Radio's *Democracy Now!* to TeleSUR, the Pan–Latin American satellite based in Venezuela) give democratic challenge to dominant media practices.

In historical review, the trend toward corporatization may be discerned early on with the formation of the Radio Corporation of America and U.S. Federal Communications Commission in the 1930s (McChesney 1993). However, the ineluctable logic of the market and its temporary triumph was most clearly codified politically with two fairly recent historic policy decisions: the *1996 Telecommunications Act* of the U.S. Congress, which removed the last obstacles to corporate consolidation of the media in the United States and the 1995 founding of the World Trade Organization, which further institutionalized the corporate media free-flow model as essential to the new world order of transnational capital. The subsequent promotion of corporate membership in the International Telecommunications Union and the dissolution of UNESCO's MacBride Roundtable on the New World Information Order organizationally confirmed the hegemony of the corporate media model (Thussu 2000). Recent decisions by the International Monetary Fund (IMF) and a score of national governments to privatize and deregulate their media, along with the increase in media joint ventures across national boundaries (Gershon 2005), confirm the trend toward a transnational media—a distinct form of globalization that brings together capitalist classes and their media in joint projects that have no national loyalty or identity in ownership, structure, or interest (see Robinson 2004).

The seventy-year wave of corporate media activity in the United States continues to mark the development of media across the continent, previewing the trajectory of international media structures, activities, and programming. Brief histories of several major U.S. media groups should illustrate the salient features of the North American model: vertical integration, concentration through mergers and acquisitions, and increasingly, joint ventures that combine multiple national media. What began as competition among media corporations seeking market dominance (and their collaborative influence on federal regulatory bodies) has plateaued with the consolidation of a handful of cooperating conglomerates seeking transnational partners. Three of the largest and most representative include the four major television networks: GE-NBC, CBS-Viacom, Disney-ABC, and Fox.

NORTH AMERICAN MAJOR MEDIA

GE-NBC

In 1919, the Radio Corporation of America (RCA) was created after the U.S. government gave the wireless industry to private investors following World War I. RCA included American Marconi (led by David Sarnoff) and many of the patents of General Electric, Westinghouse, United Fruit, and AT&T. In joint venture with GE and Westinghouse in 1926, RCA formed the National Broadcasting Corporation (NBC) and established two nationwide networks: NBC-Red and NBC-Blue. Between 1927 and 1934, the Federal Communications Commission "regulations" guaranteed commercial dominance in radio broadcasting, although GE and Westinghouse divested their interests in RCA, and RCA was forced to sell one of its national networks (which later became ABC). In 1985, GE reacquired RCA/NBC. CNBC was formed in 1989. Following the *1996 Telecommunications Act*, which removed barriers to media consolidation, NBC initiated a joint-venture cable news network (MSNBC) with Microsoft and acquired a 32 percent stake in Paxson's PAX TV network in 1999. In a joint venture with Sony and Liberty Media, NBC purchased the Spanish-language Telemundo group in 2002, in an attempt to reach part of the growing Spanish-language market in the U.S. Internationally, GE and French-based Vivendi Universal created NBC Universal, which includes theme parks, Universal Pictures, and three cable channels. From a stand-alone media giant in the 1940s and 1950s, GE's NBC has transformed into a transnational media operation that includes other major U.S., Japanese, Mexican, and French entities. For more listings of NBC holdings see www.cjr.org/tools/owners/ge.asp

CBS-Westinghouse-Viacom

Beginning with Westinghouse's first radio station, KDKA, in Pittsburgh in 1920 and William Paley's purchase of the Columbia Broadcasting System (CBS) in 1928, the evolution to the CBS-Viacom-Westinghouse media conglomerate has brought together many strands, including publishing (Simon and Schuster), radio (Infinity and American Radio), television (CBS, UPN, and King Productions), cable (MTV, Nickelodeon, BET, VH1, and many others), outdoor advertising, movie production (Paramount) and distribution (Blockbuster video), music (Sony), and the Internet. Notably, the *1996 Telecommunications Act* allowed CBS to expand its radio holdings, purchase syndicated television production studios, and through its 1999 merger with Viacom even exceed the 35 percent share of broadcast holdings officially mandated by the FCC. Viacom's U.S. and international operations include major joint ventures, including the satellite/cable network Comedy Central (jointly owned with AOL–TimeWarner until 2005), MTV Asia (with over forty million subscribers) and MTV Mandarin (jointly owned with Polygram), MTV Brazil (jointly owned with Abril), Nickelodeon UK (with BSkyB TV, a Murdoch-Fox company), VH1 Germany (with Bear-Stearns), and other projects with Vivendi Universal. Now that it has become a major global media giant, Viacom has turned toward forging transnational alliances with other major media interests from France, Australia, Brazil, and Germany, among others. Indeed, over 70 percent of all international MTV/VH1 programming is local. It would be difficult to argue that Viacom's MTV has a U.S. national identity— rather the commercial model of music promotion and celebrity chat has become globalized and localized as part of an emerging transnational class media policy. For more listings see www.cjr.org/tools/owners/viacom.asp or http://www.answers.com/topic/list-of-assets-owned-by-viacom.

ABC-Disney

The storied history of Disney began with the creation of Mickey Mouse in the 1920s. The American Broadcasting Corporation (ABC) emerged from the FCC-mandated antimonopoly sell-off of NBC-Blue in 1943. Both grew through the production and distribution of popular entertainment. Disney purchased the cable sports network ESPN in 1984 and bought Miramax in 1993 for producing more mature film fare. ABC was sold to Disney in 1996, during the heady days of media mergers erupting after the FCC's historic deregulation decisions. More than other media giants, Disney tends to go it alone in international projects, given its strong brand appeal. Yet, Disney still participates in joint ventures on occasion (e.g., a pay-per-view project with Sony-Japan and ODG in the United Kingdom; a ten-year joint-venture license agreement with Modi in India; and various corporate-government deals for Disney theme parks and hotels, as in 2005 in Hong Kong). Although Disney may not currently be a major player in the emerging transnational media formation, Disney's clear attempt to produce and market culturally diverse and internationally marketable feature animation, such as *Aladdin*, *Mulan*, *Lilo and Stitch*, and *Finding Nemo*, recognizes the cultural basis for joint venture, foreign direct investment, and transnational media product. For a list of Disney holdings, see www.cjr.org/tools/owners/disney.asp.

Fox News Corp

The *Columbia Journalism Review* summarizes the history of Murdoch's Fox by writing,

> Molded under the watchful eye of Rupert Murdoch, News Corp. continues to evolve and serve as a model for the modern vertically integrated media conglomerate. Aided by the acquisition of 20th Century film studio, News Corp. went from primarily a newspaper company in Australia and England to an influential force in American media. The Fox Network broke ground in the late 1980s as the first successful broadcast network to break through against the powerful Big 3. Recently, viewership for its Fox News Network surpassed the once formidable CNN. (*Columbia Journalism Review* 2005)

After inheriting a small daily newspaper in Australia, Rupert Murdoch acquired several others and launched Australia's first national newspaper in 1964. Murdoch expanded to the United Kingdom with the purchase of the *London Sun* in 1969. Murdoch bought the *New York Post*, the *Village Voice*, and other U.S. publications in 1977, and after buying channel 10 in Australia, formed the News Corp. in 1980. Sky TV, the first satellite station, was formed in 1983. Murdoch became a U.S. citizen in 1985 so he could purchase Twentieth Century Fox film studios and seven TV stations, which soon developed into the Fox TV network in 1986. In a 1990 merger with British Satellite Broadcasting, BSkyB TV was created in the United Kingdom. Murdoch's extensive media buying led to bankruptcy the same year, but Citibank helped organize a restructuring. After the early 1990s, Murdoch increasingly relied on mergers and investments to expand. He raised his share in the Asian satellite broadcaster, Star TV, to 63 percent. A 2003 investment in Hughes Electronics also gave News Corp. a significant holding in DirectTV, a leading direct broadcasting system in North America. Now, more than 75 percent of the globe is covered by satellite broadcasts from News Corp.'s transnational joint ventures. For a list of News Corp. holdings see www.cjr.org/tools/owners/news-corp.asp.

AOL–TimeWarner

The largest media company in the world was formed with the 2000 merger of Internet provider America Online (AOL) and the film-magazine-television corporation TimeWarner. Henry Luce's *Time* magazine and Warner Bros., Pictures Inc., were both formed in 1923, and both proceeded to grow and prosper by developing many other productions: *Fortune, Life, Sports Illustrated*; Looney Tunes, Warner Records, and more. While media entrepreneur Ted Turner formed Turner Broadcasting System (TBS) in 1979, launched Cable Network News (CNN) in 1980, and bought the MGM movie library in 1986, *Time* merged with Warner in 1989 and began the WB television network in 1995. Meanwhile, in 1991, a small Internet billboard system changed its name to America Online (AOL), went public in 1992, and had over one million subscribers by 1994. In the wake of the *1996 Telecommunications Act*, TimeWarner purchased TBS and continued to acquire, sell off, and spin off a variety of media products in magazines, music, and television. AOL's desire for media content and TimeWarner's search for media distribution led each to the $183 billion merger in 2000. Expansion continues through joint ventures sought with AT&T, Microsoft, Comcast, Google, and others. Internationally, TimeWarner was the first foreign cinema owner to hold a majority ownership in China's theater multiplexes; it formed the first-ever Sino foreign-film entertainment company, Warner China Film (with China Film Group and Hengdian Group) and plans a China-based home video replication-and-distribution business in 2005. For a list of holdings of AOL–TimeWarner, visit www.answers.com/topic/list-of-assets-owned-by-time-warner or www.pbs.org/wgbh/pages/frontline/shows/cool/giants/aoltimewarner.html.

Another dozen or so media companies are secondary players in the North America media market. In Canada, five companies control most media outlets (Winter 2002). The three biggest chains control more than 74 percent of daily circulation. The Asper family's CanWest Global controls more than 40 percent of English-language circulation, including a monopoly of the daily press in Saskatchewan, New Brunswick, Prince Edward Island, and Newfoundland. In 2000, CanWest bought up the Hollinger and Southam newspaper holdings from conservative media mogul Conrad Black. In 2001, it acquired majority control of Black's *National Post*, a Toronto-based Canada-wide daily. CanWest owns 14 large city dailies, 120 smaller dailies and weeklies, and the Global TV network, Canada's second-largest private broadcaster. The company also has private TV networks in Australia, New Zealand, and Ireland, among other holdings. The telephone company Bell Canada owns the *Globe and Mail* as well as CTV, the largest private television network; it also controls the Internet portal Sympatico. Montreal-based Quebecor owns the *Sun* newspaper chain, magazines, cable TV, the Canoe Internet portal, music and video stores, and the private TVA network in Quebec. Torstar Corporation, publisher of Harlequin romance novels, owns the *Toronto Star*, Canada's largest circulation daily, as well as 4 other dailies and 69 weeklies. Rogers Communications has interests in cable, radio, television, magazines, video stores, and wireless telephone. Additional U.S.–based media include Gannett, publisher of a chain of newspapers; the Chicago-based Tribune Company, which owns cable station WGN-TV, the *Los Angeles Times*, and other media; cable-provider Comcast; the Sinclair television group; Clear Channel, owner of 1,400 radio stations and outdoor advertising; Cumulus radio network; Liberty Media, the cable and satellite television group, which like most other mid–major media has shares in AOL, News Corp., Vivendi International, Motorola, and other major media companies. Additionally, Spanish-language media are expanding across the continent led by Grupo Televisa, the largest Spanish-language media company in the world with four networks and over 260 stations; Univisión, a joint venture which includes the Venezuelan Cisneros media group and Grupo Televisa; NBC's Telemundo network; and TV Azteca, the second-largest television network in Mexico and joint partner with the Pappas group in the U.S. TV network, Azteca America. Many of these media, especially the majors, have additional economic interests in Internet projects, professional sports teams, theme parks, franchised products, telecommunications production, and a variety of media distribution programs, such as movie distribution studios, pay-per-view channels, satellite networks, video and music rental, concert arenas and sales, and other complementary operations selling and promoting media products.

One of the distinguishing features of these commercial media, from large to small, is their almost-absolute conformity to the commercial model (Artz 2003). Unleashed from public responsibility under the cover of media deregulation in the United States and Canada, and privatization in Mexico, North American media have adhered to the corporate model of advertising-funded entertainment. While the language and appearance of actors may vary, network programming from San Juan, Puerto Rico, Chicago, Illinois, and Vancouver, British Colombia, is remarkably similar in its form and normative content. Despite the frequent lack of plot resolution on CBS's *Da Vinci's Inquest* (Duncan 2003), the program not only mirrors the urban crime storylines depicted on NBC's *Law and Order* collection, their narratives unravel with much of the same tempo and social commentary. Likewise, NBC's *Days of Our Lives* and Telemundo's *Body of Desire* may differ in the dramatic flourishes of the actors or the cultural icons of the set, but they vary little in privileging self-gratification, extremely self-centered storylines, and the promotion of familial self-reliance, marital fidelity, and stereotypical feminized romance. Game shows, news coverage, and sport telecasts reveal the same triumph of the commercial model: advertising needs are paramount in time, duration, and programming content; passive spectatorship, graphic stimulation, self-gratification, and submission to authority predominate (whether in game rules and host, expert source and news anchor, or team owner and referee). These media characteristics have not appeared magically, or out of traditional cultural practices. None of these make sense without understanding the class impulse and interest of corporate media.

MEDIA AND CLASS

Class analysis cannot explain all media activity. Recognizing the class character of media practices, processes, and structures cannot explain why *Betty La Fea* became a success in Colombia in 1999–2000, nor predict if it will be a hit for ABC in the United States in 2006. However, media practices, processes, and structures, in general, make no sense without understanding the social class relations of production (Artz 2006). Just as debates about civil society, democracy, and political reform are naïve or meaningless without reference to social class power (González 2006), so too the financing, control, creation, production, promotion, distribution, and the reception and use of the media can be confusing or misconstrued if we fail to recognize how economic interests (e.g., investments, costs, advertising, interlocking directorships, profits, etc.), political interests (e.g., regulation, market goals, power, prestige, and control rewards, etc.) and cultural interests (e.g., ideology, traditions, normative behaviors, etc.) are informed and constrained by class relations.

As countless historical accounts demonstrate, who owns and controls the media affects the production, content, and distribution of the media (e.g., Sparks 1998; Mattelart 1986; Budd and Kirsch 2005), albeit not primarily in a personal, individual sense, as whether Gannett, Black, or Murdoch own the particular station or newspaper, but more as whether the media operation is capitalist: commercial, for-profit, and advertising- and market-driven. Moreover, capitalist nation-states have a variety of social class formations, and hence a variety of media formations. The BBC system in Britain, the Berlusconis's personal media monopoly in Italy, and the consolidated media monopoly in the United States demonstrate that a capitalist social order can function with a variety of media forms. Yet, the emerging media formations suggest a new global media formation, one that is replacing or superseding all national forms, one that is marked by the collaboration among capitalist classes across national borders—a transnational media formation.

TRANSNATIONAL MEDIA

Transnational media can be distinguished from international media and multinational media by their relations of production. International media may be described as national media produced in one country and distributed to other nations—a company doing business "internationally" across national borders (e.g., Warner Bros. exporting movies to Europe). Multinational media may be understood as media that are owned by a company based in one nation, produce media product in and for other countries through corporate subsidiaries, but ownership, control, and profits remain with the national parent company (e.g., CNN-Europe). In contrast, transnational media are enterprises that produce within one nation but are jointly owned by multiple corporations from multiple nations. Media mergers, acquisitions, and foreign-direct investments have blurred the national identity of many media operations (e.g., Univisión—a U.S. network owned by the Cisneros media group in Venezuela and Mexico's Grupo Televisa network; ProSieben, a German network owned by Power Rangers producer Haim Saban, Kirchmedia, and German publisher Alex Springer).

Transnational media have no national allegiance and bring together capitalist classes from two or more nations for the purpose of producing and profiting from media commodities. Transnational media do not overcome national or cultural boundaries; indeed, they depend on and exploit the national characteristics of the appropriate national capitalist class.

Transnational media are the new defining face of capitalist media global-ization, illustrating the transnational reorganization of social class forma-tion as capitalism completes its global expansion (Robinson 2004).

Of course, capitalism has expanded from its very beginning—geographically from European nations to the Americas, Africa, and Asia, through colonialism, imperialism, and neocolonialism; and socially and politically within each nation-state through the deregulation and privati-zation of the public interest. Now, in the new millennium, with globaliza-tion, capitalism has become the first truly *world* system: capitalism has not only finally displaced all precapitalist formations, it has also completed the commodification of every meaningful instance of social life, including re-placing nation-state public institutions and responsibilities with priva-tized, for-profit operations across the board—from natural resources such as land and water to social necessities such as education and health care (Robinson 2004). A key ingredient and outcome—but not cause—of this re-structuring of capitalism has been the globalization of the corporate media hegemony and its commercial-entertainment-market model (Artz 2003). The economic, political, and cultural interests of capitalist globalization are facilitated by global corporate media, which were already integral to the capitalist system due to the ownership and interlocks among media and other corporations (e.g., GE/NBC, Westinghouse/CBS, Vivendi/Univer-sal, and the financial and organizational interconnections between all ma-jor media and other capitalist institutions, such as Citibank, Chase, Ford Foundation, Prudential, etc.) (Henwood 1989). Market-driven media par-allel and reinforce capitalist commodity production.

The triumph of the market model, and a decisive characteristic of me-dia globalization, is not simply the hegemony of form, however. Al-though, the international success of programming such as *Who Wants to Be a Millionaire?*, the World Wrestling Entertainment (WWE) franchise, and the international dominance of Hollywood's narrative realism do demonstrate the dominance of the commercial-entertainment media model. Significantly, the market model's domination from Turkey to Brazil to India represents the triumph of the commercial-entertainment form *within* nation-states. In other words, radio programming in Turkey, *telenovelas* in Brazil, and Bollywood cinema in India are not colonial or neocolonial activities or results, nor are they the consequence of cultural imperialism in the hackneyed Western-cultural-dominance sense as sim-ply the local distribution of a multinational media product. Rather, dereg-ulated, privatized, commercial entertainment media practices across the globe are the manifestation of the relations of power within most devel-oped and developing countries, a reflection of the existing social and cul-tural leadership provided by national capitalist classes and the appeal of the international capitalist media model.

The deregulation and privatization of the media conform to the strategic plan of the emerging transnational capitalist class, which insists on the removal of any public accountability or restriction on the accumulation of profit. The transnational capitalist class has emerged from decades of competition, monopoly, military actions, and technological innovation with a "free" market hubris that has been institutionalized in the World Economic Forum, the World Bank, the International Monetary Fund, codified in policy with agreements such as the North American Free Trade Agreement, and perspectives such as "The Washington Consensus," a major tract of neoliberalism and its free-market prescriptions for deregulation, privatization, and transnational development. We are witnessing the emergence of a new international social hierarchy that includes the globalization of inequality and poverty across national borders. Contrary to the postmodern claims that we have seen the end of history and the end of the nation-state, nation-states were instrumental in determining the liberalization process.

National capitalist classes politically led the privatization campaign so that national policies were reformed for the benefit of foreign direct investment, mergers, and acquisitions, while public works and social programs were financially and organizationally gutted to facilitate the privatization, the sell-off, of what had been in many cases historically national resources—including natural resources such as oil and water, and social resources such as telecommunications, public education, water, gas, transportation, and other utilities. Media were included in the deregulation/privatization frenzy of the past decade, as national markets were deregulated and then opened to foreign media products and investments, which has proved devastating to the national cinema in Europe and to broadcasting on three continents.

We must note, however, that the conflict here is not cultural or national. The false debate between cultural imperialism and cultural hybridity must be laid to rest as we recognize the hegemonic process of forging a cooperative, *transnational* capitalist class leadership. Despite some remaining intraclass competition, capitalist classes have forged new relations among themselves across national boundaries, through new transnational class institutions, which economically, politically, and socially are leading and directing national policies around the globe. The WTO dictates the rules of trade among nations. The IMF mandates national social policies as terms for international loans to developing nations. The World Economic Forum educates all national leaderships about neoliberalism and the advantages of the free market; its 100 World Media Leaders consult, edit, and advise on the free flow of information (Van der Pijl 1998). The International Telecommunications Union (ITU), formerly an international nation-state consultative and regulatory body, has recognized the new transnational class alignment and now seats corporate media as full members (Thussu 2000). The transnational capitalist class works through these new international policy and regulatory bodies; it also works through the nation-state wherever the indigenous capitalist class has hegemonic leadership.

In this process of transnational realignment, the media are being rapidly transformed. Competition has become muted among the major media, as their transnational joint interests become clear. Media are becoming transnationalized through joint ventures, foreign direct investment, and mergers. It is becoming increasingly difficult to identify the national character of the media, except through genealogy.

The deterritorialization of media production and distribution has ruptured media national characteristics. The transnational media represent the class interests, class perspectives, and class ideology of the transnational capitalist class, albeit smoothly marketed in a diversity of cultural forms. The defining characteristic of the major U.S. or UK media is not their national origin, nor the national origin of their primary shareholders, managers, or producers. The defining characteristic of the major media must be found in their class relations. Mergers and acquisitions integrate national media into the transnational media.

Among media, competition among the majors is giving way to consolidation within nations and internationally to shield investors from risk and to maximize expertise horizontally across companies. This year in the United States, for example, Sprint Nextel, Comcast, TimeWarner, Cox Communications, and Advance/Newhouse Communications formed a joint venture for video entertainment and Internet products. Others include MSNBC, the cable news channel by Microsoft and NBC; all of the other major U.S. media have entered into domestic joint ventures with each other, telecommunication producers and providers, and other industries. Each of the major media has also expanded their transnational connections through joint ventures and mergers. In addition to the ones mentioned in the profiles above, which included joint ventures by companies based in the United States, Brazil, France, China, Japan, Germany, the United Kingdom, and others, a few more joint ventures are noteworthy and should help illustrate the transnational trend:

- Sony (Japan) with Ericsson (Sweden) in cellular phones
- Sony (Japan) with Samsung (Korea) in LCD television
- Sony (Japan) with BMG (Bertelsmann-Germany) in music
- AT&T (U.S.) with UKTV (UK) in television channels
- Nickelodeon Australia (Viacom-U.S.) with News Corp. (U.S./Australia)
- Nickelodeon Germany (Viacom-U.S.) with Ravensburger and Bear Stearns (Germany)

- HBO (TimeWarner U.S.) joint ventures with Brazil, China, Hungary, others
- NBC (U.S.) joint venture with TV Azteca (Mexico)
- CNN (TimeWarner U.S.) with Cable Net (Egypt)
- Comcast (U.S.), TimeWarner (U.S.) with AIT (Nigeria) in Africa video distribution
- NBC (U.S.) and Vivendi (France) in Universal Pictures cinema
- News Corp. (U.S.) with Singapore Telecom in Internet development
- Zee (India) with MGM (TimeWarner U.S.) and Viacom (U.S.) in Internet movie channels
- Bertelsmann (Germany) with Disney/ABC (U.S.) in film/television production
- AOL (TimeWarner, U.S.) with Bertlesmann (Germany) in Internet content

Under what nation's list should we place the telecom merger of Vodafone (UK) (a joint venture partner with the French company Vivendi), Airtouch (U.S.), and Mannesmann (Germany)? What is the national identity of Germany's Vox television channel, jointly owned by Australian/American citizen Rupert Murdoch's News Corp. (49.9 percent), the French media group Canal Plus (24.9 percent), and the German-based international media giant Bertelsmann? We are at the first surge of joint ventures, as global media negotiate the best institutional and financial relations for realigning media transnationally.

Across and around this media globe, transnational media are the new media. Through the World Economic Forum, the IMF, the World Bank, and transnational policy agreements, the transnational capitalist class has politically and economically institutionalized its free-market strategy for the future of humanity. Emerging transnational media will further this institutionalization by socially and culturally advancing news, information, advertising, and entertainment, which reinforces and promotes the transnational neoliberal policies, norms, and values. Meanwhile a transnational working class also objectively exists (think GM, Nike, BP Shell, Disney, Sony, or any other capitalist enterprise that has multiple decentralized national production facilities and socially organizes thousands through a centralized just-in-time production system). Yet, this transnational working class still lives primarily on the national level, politically constrained by national borders, laws, and state-enforced coercion, and socially susceptible to nationalism, patriotism, and localism—all available via transnational media for domestic consumption and profit. Indeed, transnational media are the perfect vehicles for mass persuasion, organization, and distraction, because they escape the scrutiny of cultural difference, benefit from the national identity of the domestic capitalist partner, and produce a culturally familiar entertainment product with the best media production expertise possible.

Transnational media, initiated and led largely by U.S. media, are the new hegemony, providing leadership and organization for the transnational capitalist class and for all world citizens. While independent media and public media provide a valuable antidote (and Qatar's Al-Jazeera and Venezuela's TeleSUR, the Pan–Latin American network, suggest possibilities for publicly accessible media), transnational media are the ultimate in deregulation, privatization, and commercialization: smooth, clear, and pleasing in their promotion of the corporate media model. Citizens of the world, rejoice! Transnational media will soon deliver via more than two hundred channels the best in individual gratification, audience narrowcasting, consumerism, authoritarianism, spectatorship, distraction, and mediated passivity.

APPENDIX: WHO OWNS WHAT?

This list was compiled in part from *Columbia Journalism Review* 2005 online reports.

1. Disney

Broadcasting
(includes the Capital City/ABC subsidiary)
Television
ABC Television Network
10 owned and operated television stations
56 radio stations
Cable Television
ABC Family
The Disney Channel
Toon Disney
SoapNet
ESPN Inc. (80 percent, Hearst Corporation owns the remaining 20 percent, includes ESPN, ESPN2, ESPN News, ESPN Now, ESPN Extreme)
Classic Sports Network
A&E Television (37.5 percent, with Hearst and GE)
The History Channel (with Hearst and GE)
Lifetime Television (50 percent, with Hearst)
Lifetime Movie Network (50 percent with Hearst)
E! Entertainment (with Comcast and Liberty Media)
International Broadcast
The Disney Channel UK
The Disney Channel Taiwan
The Disney Channel Australia

The Disney Channel Malaysia
The Disney Channel France
The Disney Channel Middle East
The Disney Channel Italy
The Disney Channel Spain
ESPN Inc. International Ventures
Sportsvision of Australia (25 percent)
ESPN Brazil (50 percent)
ESPN STAR (50 percent, sports programming throughout Asia)
Net STAR (33 percent, owners of The Sports Network of Canada)
Other International Ventures (all with minority ownership)
Tele-Munchen (German television production and distribution)
RTL-2 (German television production and distribution)
Hamster Productions (French television production)
TV Sport of France
Tesauro of Spain
Scandinavian Broadcasting System
Japan Sports Channel
Television Production and Distribution
Buena Vista Television
Touchstone Television
Walt Disney Television
Walt Disney Television Animation (has three wholly owned production facilities
    outside the United States—Japan, Australia, Canada)
Movie Production and Distribution
Walt Disney Pictures
Touchstone Pictures
Hollywood Pictures
Caravan Pictures
Miramax Films
Buena Vista Home Video
Buena Vista Home Entertainment
Buena Vista International
Theme Parks and Resorts
Other
TiVo (partial investment)
Hyperion Books and magazines

2. General Electric

NBC Universal (80 percent owned by GE, 20 percent controlled by Vivendi Universal)
Television
14 owned and operated NBC stations
14 owned and operated Telemundo stations
NBC Universal Television Studio
NBC Universal Television Distribution

CNBC
MSNBC
Bravo
Mun2TV
Sci-Fi
Trio
USA
Film
Universal Pictures
Parks
Universal Parks and Resorts
Other
Paxson Communications (30 percent)

3. Liberty Media

Subscription Television
Court TV (50 percent)
Discovery Communications Inc. (50 percent)
Discovery Channel
The Learning Channel
Animal Planet
Travel Channel
Discovery Health Channel
Discovery Civilization
Discovery Home and Leisure
Discovery Kids
Discovery Science
Discovery Wings
People and Arts
Europe Showcase
E! Entertainment Television (10 percent)
Style
QVC
Starz Encore Group (100 percent)
Game Show Network (50 percent)
MacNeil/Lehrer Productions (67 percent)
DMX Music
International Channel (90 percent)
Jupiter Programming Co. (Japan) (50 percent)
Pramer S.C.A. (Argentina) (100 percent)
The Premium Movie Partnership (Australia) (20 percent)
Torneos y Competencias, S.A. (40 percent)
Cable and Telephony
Cablevisión S.A. (Argentina) (39 percent)
Chorus Communications Limited (Ireland) (40 percent)
Digital Latin America (43 percent)

IDT Corporation (11 percent)
Jupiter Telecommunications Co. (Japan) (45 percent)
Liberty Cablevision of Puerto Rico Inc. (100 percent)
Metrópolis-Intercom, S.A. (Chile) (50 percent)
Omnipoint Communications Inc. (4 percent)
Sprint PCS Group (20 percent)
Telewest Communications (UK) (20 percent)
The Wireless Group (30 percent)
UnitedGlobalCom Inc. (74 percent)
Satellite Communications Services
Liberty Satellite and Technology Inc. (87 percent)
Aerocast.com Inc. (39 percent)
Astrolink International LLC (27 percent)
Hughes Electronics Corporation (1 percent)
On Command Corporation (66 percent)
Sky Latin America Satellite (9 percent)
Wildblue Communications Inc. (32 percent)
XM Satellite Radio Holdings Inc. (1 percent)
Other
AOL TimeWarner Inc. (4 percent)
News Corporation (17 percent)
Viacom (1 percent)
Vivendi Universal (4 percent)
PRIMEDIA (partial investment)
Motorola Inc. (3 percent)
Cendant Corporation (3 percent)

4. Fox News/Murdoch

Television
Fox Broadcasting Company
35 Fox Television Stations
DBS and Cable
FOXTEL
BSkyB
Star
DIRECTV
Sky Italia
Fox News Channel
Fox Movie Channel
FX
FUEL
National Geographic Channel
SPEED Channel
Fox Sports Net
FSN New England (50 percent)
FSN Ohio

FSN Florida
National Advertising Partners
Fox College Sports
Fox Soccer Channel
Stats Inc.
Film
Twentieth Century Fox
Fox Searchlight Pictures
Fox Television Studios
Blue Sky Studios
Dozens of Newspapers and Magazines in the United States, United Kingdom, and
    Australia
Harper Morrow Book Publishers
Other
Los Angeles Kings (NHL, 40 percent option)
Los Angeles Lakers (NBA, 9.8 percent option)
Staples Center (40 percent owned by Fox/Liberty)
News Interactive
Fox Sports Radio Network
Sky Radio Denmark
Sky Radio Germany
Broadsystem
Classic FM
Festival Records
Fox Interactive
IGN Entertainment
Mushroom Records
MySpace.com
National Rugby League
NDS
News Outdoor
Nursery World
Scout Media

5. Sony

Film
Sony Pictures Entertainment
Columbia TriStar
Sony Pictures Classics
Screen Gems
Television
Sony Pictures Television
AXN
Animax Japan
SoapCity
GAME SHOW NETWORK (50 percent with Liberty Media)

Movielink (jointly owned with Paramount Pictures, Sony Pictures Entertainment, Universal Studios, and Warner Bros. Studios)

Music

Sony BMG Music Entertainment (50 percent with Bertelsmann) Labels include: Arista Records, BMG Classics, BMG Heritage, BMG International Companies, Columbia Records, Epic Records, J Records, Jive Records, LaFace Records, Legacy Recordings, RCA Records, RCA Victor Group, RLG - Nashville, Sony Classical, Sony Music International, Sony Music Nashville, Sony Wonder, So So Def Records, Verity Records

Sony/ATV Music Publishing (joint venture with Michael Jackson)

Music Choice (venture with TimeWarner, EMI, Motorola, Microsoft, and several cable companies: Cox, Comcast, Adelphia, TimeWarner Cable)

Other

Sony Electronics

Sony Computer Entertainment America

PlayStation

989 Sports

Sony Connect Inc.

Metreon

6. TimeWarner

TimeWarner Book Group

TimeWarner Book Group UK

TimeWarner Audio Books

Time Inc.

Warner Books

Little, Brown and Company

Cable

HBO

CNN

CNN International

CNN en Espanol

CNN Headline News

CNN Airport Network

CNN fn

CNN Radio

CNN Interactive

Court TV (with Liberty Media)

TimeWarner Cable

Road Runner

New York 1 News (24-hour news channel devoted only to NYC)

Kablevision (53.75 percent, cable television in Hungary)

TimeWarner Inc. Film and TV Production/Distribution

Warner Bros.

Warner Bros. Studios

Warner Bros. Television (production)

The WB Television Network
Warner Bros. Television Animation
Hanna-Barbera Cartoons
Telepictures Production
Witt-Thomas Productions
Castle Rock Entertainment
Warner Home Video
Warner Bros. Domestic Pay-TV
Warner Bros. Domestic Television Distribution
Warner Bros. International Television Distribution
The Warner Channel (Latin America, Asia, Pacific, Australia, Germany)
Warner Bros. International Theaters (owns/operates multiplex theaters in over 12
   countries)
Magazines, Books, and Comics
Online Services
CompuServe Interactive Services
AOL Instant Messenger
AOL.com portal
Digital City
AOL Europe
ICQ
The Knot Inc. (wedding content; 8 percent with QVC 36 percent and Hummer)
WinbladFunds (18 percent)
MapQuest.com (pending regulatory approval)
Spinner.com
Winamp
DrKoop.com (10 percent)
Legend (49 percent, Internet service in China)
Theme Parks
Warner Brothers Recreation Enterprises (owns/operates international theme
   parks)
Entertainment Networks
TBS Superstation
Turner Network Television (TNT)
Turner South
Cartoon Network
Turner Classic Movies
Cartoon Network in Europe
Cartoon Network in Latin America
TNT and Cartoon Network in Asia/Pacific
Film Production
New Line Cinema
Fine Line Features
Turner Original Productions
Sports
Atlanta Braves

Other
Netscape Communications
Netscape Netcenter portal
AOL MovieFone
iAmaze
Amazon.com (partial)
Quack.com
Streetmail (partial)
Switchboard (6 percent)

7. Viacom

Television
18 CBS Stations
18 UPN Stations
5 Other Stations
Cable
MTV
MTV2
Nickelodeon
BET
Nick at Nite
TV Land
NOGGIN
VH1
Spike TV
CMT
Comedy Central
Showtime
The Movie Channel
Flix
Sundance Channel
Television Production and Distribution
Spelling Television
Big Ticket Television
King World Productions
Infinity Broadcasting 150+ Radio Stations
Viacom Outdoor Group
Film
Paramount Pictures
Paramount Home Entertainment
Publishing
Simon and Schuster

REFERENCES

Artz, L. (2003). "Globalization, media hegemony, and social class." In L. Artz and Y. Kamalipour (eds.), *The globalization of corporate media hegemony*, pp. 3–31. Albany: State University of New York.

—— (2006). "On the material and the dialectic: Toward a class analysis of communication." In L. Artz, S. Macek, and D. Cloud, (eds)., *Marxism and communication: The point is to change it.* New York: Peter Lang.

Budd, M., and Kirsch, M. H., eds. (2005). *Rethinking Disney: Private control, public dimensions.* Middletown, Conn.: Wesleyan University.

Duncan, G. (2003, November 5). "Sick of American drama? Try *Da Vinci's Inquest.*" From *TeeVee.* At www.teevee.org/archive/2003/11/05/ (accessed online, October 15, 2005).

Gershon, R. (2005). "The transnationals." In A. Cooper-Chen (ed.), *Global entertainment media: Content, audiences, issues*, pp. 17–38. Mahwah, N.J.: Lawrence Erlbaum.

González, J.L.A. (2006, January). "Cuban civil society." *NACLA Report on the Americas* 39(4), pp. 32–37.

Henwood, D. (1989, March–December). *Extra!* series on media 2(5)–3(3).

Mattelart, A., ed. (1986). *Communicating in popular Nicaragua.* New York: International General.

McChesney, R. W. (1993). *Telecommunications, mass media, and democracy: The battle for control of U.S. broadcasting, 1928–1935.* New York: Oxford University.

Robinson, W. I. (2004). *A theory of global capitalism: Production, class, and state in a transnational world.* Baltimore: Johns Hopkins.

Sparks, C. (1998). *Communism, capitalism, and the mass media.* London: Sage.

Thussu, D. (2000). *International communication.* London: Arnold.

Van der Pijl, K. (1998). *Transnational classes and international relations.* London: Routledge.

Winter, J. (2002, May–June). "Canada's media monopoly." *Extra!* At www.fair.org/index.php?page=1106 (accessed October 15, 2005).

Index

Note: Page references in *italics* indicate illustrations or tables.

About the Contributors

Lee Artz is associate professor in the Department of Communication and Creative Arts at Purdue University Calumet, where he is director of the Center for Instructional Excellence. Artz has published many book chapters and journal articles on international media, cultural diversity, and democratic communication. He is author of *Cultural hegemony in the United States* (2000) and coeditor of *Marxism and communication studies: The point is to change it* (2006), *Bring `em on! Media and politics in the Iraq War* (2004), *The globalization of corporate media hegemony* (2003), *Public media and the public interest* (2002), and *Communication and democratic society* (2001).

Lyombe Eko is associate professor in the School of Journalism and Mass Communication at the University of Iowa. He teaches media law and ethics, comparative and international communication, and documentary video production. Eko has published articles in *Communication Law and Policy, Loyola International and Comparative Law Review, International Journal of Communication Law and Policy, Communications and the Law, The International Journal of Comic Art, The Journal of Black Studies*, and the *Journal of Third World Studies*. He has also contributed to several books and encyclopedias. Eko was also a journalist and award-winning producer for the African Broadcasting Union (URTNA) in Nairobi, Kenya, and at Cameroon Radio and Television Corporation, Cameroon, West Africa.

Cees J. Hamelink studied philosophy and psychology in Amsterdam. He is professor emeritus of International Communication at the University of Amsterdam and professor of Globalization, Human Rights, and Health at the Vrije Universiteit in Amsterdam. Hamelink has worked as a journalist as well as a consultant on media and communication policy for several international organizations and national governments. He is currently the editor-in-chief of the *International Journal for Communication Studies: Gazette*, past president of the International Association for Media and Communication Research, president of the Dutch Federation for Human Rights, founder of the People's Communication Charter, and board member of the international news agency Inter Press Service. Professor Hamelink has guest-lectured in over 40 countries and has published over 250 articles, papers, and chapters in academic publications. Among the 16 books he has authored are *World communication* (1995), *The ethics of cyberspace* (2000), and *Human rights for communicators* (2004). Forthcoming is a book on political ethics and communication.

Yahya R. Kamalipour is professor and head of the Department of Communication and Creative Arts at Purdue University Calumet. He has taught at universities in Ohio, Illinois, Missouri, Indiana, Oxford (England), and Tehran (Iran). His most recent coedited books are *Bring 'em on! Media and politics in the Iraq War* (2004); *War, media, and propaganda* (2004); *The globalization of corporate media hegemony* (2004); *Global communication* (2002); and *Media, sex, violence, and drugs in the global village*. He is the founder and managing editor of *Global Media Journal* (www.globalmedia-journal.com) and coeditor (with K. R. Rampal) of the State University of New York Press series in Global Media Studies.

Joe F. Khalil has more than ten years of professional television experience as director, executive producer, and consultant with CNBC Arabiya, MBC, MTV, and Orbit. For seven years, he was an instructor at the Lebanese American University, where his teaching and research focused on transnational broadcasting, programming, and production. His writings have been presented at several conferences and he has consulted for academic and professional organizations on media in the Middle East.

Alan Knight is chair of Journalism and Media Studies at Central Queensland University and president of its academic board. Knight is a former journalist employed by the Australian Broadcasting Corporation, Australian Associated Press, and Radio Television Hong Kong. He was appointed an Honorary Research Fellow at the Centre for Asian Studies at Hong Kong University in 1994 and is a board member of the Asian Media Information Research Centre (Singapore) and the Australian Centre for Independent Journalism. He writes and researches foreign correspondence, new media, radical publishing, and postcolonial journalism.

Marwan M. Kraidy is assistant professor of International Relations and International Communication at American University in Washington, D.C., and an expert on Arab media. He is the author of *Hybridity, or the cultural logic of globalization* (Temple 2005) and coeditor of *Global media studies: Ethnographic perspectives* (Routledge 2003). Kraidy has authored many articles in leading journals. He is completing his current book, *Screens of contention: Arab media and the challenges of modernity*, as a 2005–2006 Fellow at the Woodrow Wilson International Center for Scholars in Washington, D.C.

José-Carlos Lozano is director of the Center for Communication Research, Monterrey Institute of Technology, Mexico, and a former director of Mexico on the Executive Board of the Federation of Latin American Communication Schools. A member of the National System of Researchers, of the National Council for Science and Technology of Mexico, he is also the author of numerous books and journal articles in the areas of mass, political, and international communication. Lozano is former editor of the *Mexican communication yearbook, volumes 1–4*, and was TELE-VISA chair at the Monterrey Institute of Technology, where he directed a massive, quantitative, and qualitative reception study in Mexico City, Guadalajara, and Monterrey. Currently, he holds the Audiovisual Media and Globalization in North America chair at the Monterrey Institute of Technology.

Kuldip R. Rampal is professor of Mass Communication at Central Missouri State University in Warrensburg. A widely published author, Rampal received the 1993 International Communication Award from the Republic of China on Taiwan for his writings on press and political liberalization in Taiwan. Rampal has coauthored the reference book *International Afro mass media: A reference guide* (1996) and coedited *Media, sex, violence and drugs in the global village* (2001). He is coeditor (with Y. Kamalipour) of the State University of New York Press series in Global Media Studies.

Jeanette Steemers is principal lecturer in Television Studies at the School of Media and Cultural Production, De Montfort University, Leicester, England. She is author of *Selling television: British television in the global marketplace* (2004), coauthor of *European television industries* (2005), and coeditor of the international journal *Convergence: The Journal of Research into New Media Technologies*. She is currently undertaking a two-year Arts and Humanities Research Council–funded project on the Production Ecology of Preschool Television in Britain.